NEW THEATRE
FORMS

# NEW
# THEATRE FORMS

BY
STEPHEN JOSEPH

THEATRE ARTS BOOKS
New York

*First published* 1968

THEATRE ARTS BOOKS
333 Sixth Avenue, New York 10014

Library of Congress Catalog Card Number 68–13407

MADE IN GREAT BRITAIN AT THE PITMAN PRESS, BATH

# FOREWORD

By Percy Corry

IT is often argued that the proscenium stage does not best meet the needs of contemporary theatre. Many argue from profound conviction: many more accept the argument because they are afraid of being thought reactionary: even more would be quite surprised to learn that anybody should wish to have any different form of theatre. It is probably in the educational fields of drama that one finds the greatest interest in alternatives to the proscenium stage. This may be significant.

Stephen Joseph has had considerable experience of theatre of various forms. For many years he pioneered professional theatre in the round in this country. In doing so he has often been exasperated into deliberate exaggeration of its virtues by cynical opposition or by apathetic conservatism. He is a vigorous iconoclast with the courage of his convictions: at considerable personal sacrifice he put theories into practice. Even those who may disagree with his arguments or with his conclusions may not doubt his integrity or his knowledge of what he is talking about.

In this book Stephen Joseph approaches the problems provocatively but objectively, reasonably and lucidly: he states his case in practical terms. The reader who is quite determined that his own convictions will remain unshaken must respect the argument, which cannot be refuted lightly. An occasional note of pessimistic disillusion may be detected: Joseph has long been an enthusiastic prophet crying in the wilderness and his innate modesty occasionally misleads him to under-estimate the influence of his liberal casting of pearls.

This is a book that will be interesting and informative to anybody who has a keen concern for the theatre.

# PREFACE

PERHAPS this book should have contained an orderly description of each new form of theatre, and the chapter headings may give the impression that it does so; but in fact the new forms of theatre have all sorts of things in common, and I take them up whenever the opportunity arises.

This may disappoint anyone in search of a technical dictionary, but I hope it will make for more enjoyable reading.

The origins of the book go back to a grant awarded to me by the Elmgrant Trust. This was intended to enable me to visit America with a camera, and record the new theatre buildings I found there.

One result of the visit was the mounting of an exhibition: "New Theatres In The U.S.A." This exhibition was displayed first at the Scarborough Library Theatre, and later in York during a conference of theatre architects. (It had been intended that the conference should be held regularly, but this was made unnecessary by the founding of the Association of British Theatre Technicians.)

Before starting out on the trip I had made contact with the directors of several theatres, such as the Alley Theatre in Houston, Texas, and the Arena Theatre in Washington. On arriving in New York I was urged by my friends in the theatre there not to waste my time travelling all over the country. According to them the only place to study theatre was in New York, because, as far as they knew, there was no theatre worth mentioning anywhere else. In fact once I had left New York the visit became a breathless tour of investigation. At each theatre I visited, I was given information about another, until I had a list of forty to fifty theatres. Most of these were connected with university or amateur theatre, but all of them were serving a good local purpose, and it was surprising that they were not better known in New York. However, even now most of them (and what they have achieved) are completely unknown in this country. Ideas for new theatres may seem wildly revolutionary here, whereas such theatres are in everyday use in America without our being aware of them. So one object of this book is to help, perhaps rather late in the day, to give a general introduction to some of the working examples actually in operation.

Some time after my American visit The Strand Electric Company, which publishes the magazine *Tabs* and also a number of technical publications of a more particular nature, asked me to write a booklet on the design and lighting of new forms of theatre. The preparation of this booklet made me organize my information and thinking on this subject. Obviously the booklet had to be short and succinct, whereas the subject calls for much more expansive treatment. However I hope the Strand Electric booklet remains useful, particularly on lighting control, dealt with here only in an elementary way.

Alan Barlow has been helpful in providing, after much discussion, the imaginative drawings, and I am grateful to many people who have supplied me with illustrative material, especially Mr. Beaumont-Newhall of George Eastman House for finding the plan and section of the diorama in Paris built by Daguerre.

The author gratefully acknowledges permission to reprint drawings from the following sources: On page 27 the drawing of King's College Chapel comes from *Shakespeare's Wooden O* by Leslie Hotson, (Ruper Hart-Davis, 1959); the designs by Norman Bel Geddes on pages 33, 78, 80, and 81, are from *Horizons* by Norman Bel Geddes (Little, Brown & Company, 1932); these are now among the drawings in the Bel Geddes Collection at the University of Texas. The drawings on page 53 and the photograph reproduced as plate viii of the Olathe High School were supplied by the Architects, Shaver and Company; the drawings of the Theatre in the Park on page 54 by the Architect, Hugh Hardy, associate architect Herman Shapiro; the drawing of the Festival Theatre, Cambridge, on page 69 is reproduced from *Stage Lighting* by Harold Ridge, published by Heffer, Cambridge, 1928; the drawings on pages 84 and 85 are from *The Open Stage* by James Hull Miller, published by the Hub Electric Company; the drawing of Daguerre's Diorama on page 90 is reproduced by permission of the Curator, Gernsheim Collection, at the University of Texas; the drawing of the John F. Kennedy Center was supplied by the Architect, Edward Durrell Stone; the drawing of the tilting floor on page 104 and the diagrams to illustrate the sightlines formula were supplied by Messrs. Watts and Corry. The extract on page 55 from *Will Shakespeare* by Clemence Dane is quoted by permission of Messrs. Heinemann Educational Ltd.

In selecting illustrative material I have been greatly helped by the Editors of *Progressive Architecture* and *Tabs* magazine.

In the later stages of preparation of this book, I fell seriously ill, and was given substantial help by David Campton with the text and by Percy Corry with the illustrations. In the whole preparation of the book, the publishers have been more than usually helpful.

STEPHEN JOSEPH

# CONTENTS

# LIST OF PLATES

*(Between pages 64 and 65)*

# ILLUSTRATIONS IN TEXT

*Drawings by Alan Barlow*

# I

## INTRODUCTORY

A THEATRE is a complicated building, and it will probably have an interesting life story, including many structural alterations, redecorations outside and in, and the putting in of new equipment, as well as many changes of name. For instance, the Adelphi Theatre in the Strand started in 1806 as the Sans Pareil, became the Adelphi in 1819, and the Theatre Royal, Adelphi, in 1829. It was then rebuilt and opened as the Theatre Royal, New Adelphi, in 1858. From 1867 it was called the Royal Adelphi Theatre. The third version, opened in 1901, was called the Century Theatre, but in the following year the name again reverted to the Royal Adelphi Theatre. A fourth theatre was opened in 1930, and the "Royal" was dropped from the name in 1940. This is the bare bones of the story and the changes in name are no more than hints. Many other alterations were made, and a summary of them can be found in *The Theatres of London*[1]; the first theatre listed in the book serves as my example.

If you examine a theatre with a history of this kind it is difficult to say precisely when the existing structure was built; it has been changed so often.

The Theatre Royal, Drury Lane, dates back to 1663, though the present structure belongs mainly to the rebuilding of 1812 and the interior to 1946, with even more recent alteration. Incidentally, this theatre is not, and never has been, in Drury Lane. It backs on to Drury Lane, with its front portico in what was once Bridges Street and is now Catherine Street. The point is worth making to serve as a warning that we are dealing with material of an intractable nature, not only as regards dating the structure but also where placing it, describing it, and assessing its value are concerned. This seems common to nearly all theatrical affairs. Facts have often been mislaid or have become confused, leaving plenty of room for

---

[1] Raymond Mander and Joe Mitchenson, *The Theatres of London* (Rupert Hart-Davis, London, 1961).

I

the development of traditional myth and the canonization of
opinion. Most of us who write about the theatre let our
enthusiasm colour the facts. Such deviations from absolute
truth are oftener easy to perceive in another writer than in
oneself, and I must make my apologies in advance for parading
opinion as fact and for being ignorant of relevant facts known

PRIMITIVE THEATRE

No one knows how the theatre began. Indeed its origins were many and
various. This drawing suggests how a primitive dance-drama might
have been performed.

to others. I do not intend to deceive anyone, and certainly not
myself. If I do so, my excuse is that I am in good company.

Drury Lane can claim to be our oldest theatre. Three
London theatres have their origins from the eighteenth century:
Her Majesty's, the Haymarket, and Covent Garden. A fourth,
the Lyceum, though still standing, has not been regularly used
as a theatre since 1945.

Allardyce Nicholl lists a dozen theatres in London during the
second half of the eighteenth century.[1] These include the

[1] Allardyce Nicholl, *A History of English Drama 1750 to 1800* (Cambridge
University Press, 1937).

Pantheon, an opera house that lasted two years before being burned down; Astley's, at this time almost exclusively used for equestrian shows; and Sadler's Wells, still only a room for musical entertainments and pantomime. In contrast, the list for the second half of the nineteenth century names over a hundred theatres in London, besides forty odd music halls selected as being the principal houses.[1] During the nineteenth century, and particularly towards the end of it, theatre building proceeded at a terrific rate. Building and rebuilding continued into the first decades of the twentieth century, but the pace slowed down and then came almost to a halt in face of competition from the cinema and as a result of the effects of World War I. Mander and Mitchenson, writing in the middle of the twentieth century, deal with sixty-five theatres in London, including half a dozen that have been turned into cinemas or put to other use. The theatre boom has come and gone with a vengeance. Of West-end theatres still in use, fifteen belong to the nineteenth century, fifteen to the first two decades of the twentieth century, and another dozen come almost together round the year 1930. Since then few theatres of size and significance have been built, and of these the Royalty and the Prince Charles have both become cinemas, leaving only the Mermaid and the Mayfair to represent mid-century building.

It is not enough to look at London alone, however, though where the provinces are concerned the relevant dates have nowhere been systematically compiled. If we judge by the style of architecture and general arrangement, the bigger provincial theatres seem to belong mostly to the latter part of the nineteenth century or the early part of the twentieth. This is what we would expect. There are exceptions, of course. The Theatre Royal in Bristol dates back to 1766 and the new Nottingham Playhouse was opened in 1964. Allardyce Nicholl lists 358 theatres for the second half of the nineteenth century in provincial England and Ireland.

A complication in dating arises from a very large number of provincial theatres having been made out of other buildings. But during this entire period, from the eighteenth century to the middle of the twentieth, most of these theatres, in London

[1] Allardyce Nicholl, *A History of English Drama 1850 to 1900*, Vol. I (Cambridge University Press, 1946).

and in the provinces, were built in more or less the same form
or pattern.

At the risk of seeming pedantic it is worth trying to describe
this familiar pattern, and to account for it: because of the large
number of examples many people take it so much for granted
that they assume it is the natural form of theatre, an attitude

GREEK THEATRE

At the time of Aeschylus the theatre in Greece was probably still very
simple, the only technical requirement being a hillside to give the audience good sightlines.

nicely summed up by those who, when discussing the new
forms of theatre, refer to this as the "proper" theatre.

In plan, the "proper" theatre is divided into two important
areas. One of these is the stage area, and the other is the
auditorium; and they are placed side by side so that an arch-
way, made in the wall that is shared by both volumes, provides
a communicating way between them. Seats, arranged in rows
facing the arch, allow the audience to see into the stage area,
of which they in fact only see a portion limited by the width

of the arch in the stage wall and by the use of scenery which masks off the sides and, usually, the back of the stage area. The area actually seen is where the actors perform, and it is called the acting area; the remainder is referred to as the wings and backstage. In section, the stage area is a large

ROMAN THEATRE

Huge stone theatres were built for circuses and other spectacular shows, but plays were most likely presented in more modest buildings. The drawing takes a hint from the well-known illustration to a fifteenth century edition of the plays of Terence.

rectangular structure, while the auditorium is made up of a number of floors, sloped so that the audience can see the stage; the stage is raised above the lowest level of the auditorium, and an orchestra pit often separates the two. The large volume of the stage can be complicated by various devices. The stage itself is either flat or raked, i.e. sloping gently upwards away from the arch. It may be equipped with lifts so that sections of the acting area or the whole of it can be raised and lowered, with wagons to run the acting area to one side or another, or with a revolve to turn the acting area round. Over the stage a grid of steel girders forms a ceiling: its height above the stage is at least twice as high as the vertical opening of the arch. Over the grid runs a series of pulleys, the lines from which are either tied off on a gallery or are connected to a series of counter-weights running in vertical tracks that are ranged along a side wall. These devices serve one purpose. They are there to facilitate scene changes. The proper theatre is essentially a scenic theatre.

The word "proscenium" has many meanings; it derives from the Greek, and at one time it meant a raised platform for acting on. It can be noticed in this sense in the famous Swan drawing, where the platform stage is labelled "proscenium." It retained this meaning when the Italian theatre developed the scenic area behind a frame which itself became the pro-scenium arch; the curtain in the frame is often called the proscenium curtain. In general the word has now become associated with the particular form of scenic theatre with separated stage and auditorium, which may sensibly be called the proscenium theatre. Perhaps a better term for the arch is picture-frame, which certainly has been much used. Because the stage area is enclosed by four walls it is sometimes referred to as an enclosed stage and, as we shall soon want to contrast it with another form of stage that will be called the open stage, this is a good term to adopt. We now arrive at a description that can be summarized by stating that the proscenium theatre is characterized by having an enclosed stage upon which actors and scenery are seen from the auditorium through a picture-frame. The basic function of this form of theatre, from an architectural point of view, is to house an audience that will watch actors who perform within a variable scenic world.

Few people would want to question the notion of a theatre that housed an audience so that they could watch actors performing: the element that needs further examination is the variable scenic world.

There are three related points that must be mentioned at once about the scenic world. Firstly, the origin of this form of theatre can be traced back to the Italian Renaissance when a theatrical entertainment would consist mainly of the skilful

manipulation of scenic pictures. This arose out of the human-
istic desire to come to grips with nature, and to represent it
more completely than in a painting; and to go beyond nature,
creating an imagined world as convincingly, as really, as
possible. In the case of a painting, the artist perceives an
image which he captures and transfixes, with the aid of colour
and by the art of perspective, on a flat surface. But the great

BOOTH STAGE

In the middle ages plays were performed at fairs, in market places and
whenever an audience might be found ready to contribute a few pence.

artists wanted also to capture, and depict, movement. It could
not be done on a flat surface. The images on a table of a
camera obscura were tantalizingly there to tempt them, but
they could not control these images. Their solution was a
compromise. A series of flat surfaces were used. These could
be arranged behind a picture-frame, with hidden machinery
to effect the movement. It would be wrong to suggest that the
results were hailed by renaissance painters and their patrons
as a new and significant form of art. But the moving pictures
provided entertainment for aristocratic employers and, from

the Renaissance to the middle of the nineteenth century,
artists continued to explore the possibilites of reproducing
movement in nature; photography eventually provided the
means, and cinema the outlet. Renaissance moving pictures
were housed in specially made theatres: places for seeing. The
theatrical implications are obvious. But note that the scenic
theatre originated without reference to actors: they were
brought in to fill in the gaps between scene changes (though
they were to steal the picture soon enough). The point I have
made here has been fully dealt with by Professor Kernodle.[1]
It leads immediately to my second point.

When at last it became possible to fix the image that appeared
in the camera obscura, a new way of presenting moving pictures
was devised: by projection that produced shadows. As an
entertainment it became very widespread in Europe and
America in the early years of the twentieth century and very
popular. Places in which to show the movies were already to
hand. Theatres devised to show the moving pictures of the
Renaissance were common all over Europe, and their essential
form had hardly changed, except to become bigger. Naturally,
then, an enormous number of playhouses became cinemas.
New buildings for the movies could be built without large
stage areas but otherwise they were very much the same as
existing theatres. They were called by such names as the
Electric Theatre, or the Picture Palace, which proclaimed their
function as well as their ancestry. In America the word
"theatre" has remained attached to the movie house, and
sometimes in discussion it is necessary to refer to the "live
theatre" in order to distinguish it from the movie house, which
is a "shadow theatre." The shadows were able to present more
easily to their audience the impression of nature in motion, and
certainly the more spectacular aspects of nature. The cinema
presented, then, a vigorous challenge to one of the main
attractions of the theatre.

Later, when television had further encroached on this
ground, it became important to consider if the theatre might
not do better by paying less attention to the pictures and more
to the living actor. This point is still very much under discussion. The discussion has led to action, one aspect of which

[1] George R. Kernodle, *From Art to Theatre* (Illinois, Chicago, 1943).

provides my third point. If moving scenery is to be less used in the playhouse, clearly the design of the stage can be modified so that it occupies less space. But most attempts to do this have not, so far, proved satisfactory. Of course the whole design of the playhouse might be reconsidered; and this turns out to be a more fruitful enterprise and results in new theatre forms. To

TUDOR ENTERTAINMENTS

On festival and holidays the large dining hall was turned into a theatre as soon as the meal was over.

set beside the description of the proscenium theatre already given, these new forms of theatre can be characterized by their having the acting area and the auditorium in the same architectural volume. The same four walls, as it were, form a single room in which actors and audience get together. This is a different idea from the proscenium theatre. It suggests that we should call the acting area an open stage, as opposed to an enclosed stage.

During the twenty years or so in which modern open stages have been used, three main forms have evolved. If you think of the theatre as a room with four walls, the rectangular area may have the open stage at one end, with the audience arranged in the remainder of the room, looking towards the stage. This is the end stage. Or the rectangular space may have the stage against one wall, jutting out so that the audience is spread on three sides of it; a thrust stage. Finally, if the open stage is in the middle of the room, with the audience all the way round, we have a central stage. The sequence from end stage to thrust stage and to centre stage is one in which the audience increasingly embraces the acting area. In fact the plans need not be rectangular, and they seldom are. Open stages may be a variety of shapes. A helpful way of describing each kind of open stage might be to note the different angles at which the seats are set with reference to the stage and to each other. You can call a halt anywhere in the embracing motion and devise a form of open stage, and although I have pointed to three main forms, an unlimited number of variations is available. I aim to make simple descriptions and must therefore attempt to simplify what may really become very complicated ideas. Even for our three main forms the seats at the extreme sides will usually be set at the greatest angle to each other in any form of theatre, and, taking this angle, the least difference will be for the end stage, the thrust stage will have an angle of 180° or more, and the central stage a full 360° (it is called theatre in the round because the audience is all the way round, and not because of the shape of the stage or the theatre).

This introduces the open stage as simply as possible. But even the division between enclosed and open stages is not always precise. However, differences exist and the distinctions are worth making because each kind of theatre has its special qualities. If we look at these qualities and characteristics at an elementary level, it should be all the easier to proceed with a proper analysis of more sophisticated examples. And, what is important, it is worth having and using small theatres, modestly designed and equipped, to prepare us for the proper use of larger and better theatres. More important still, most modern theatres of no matter what form are badly designed and equipped because elementary principles have not been grasped by client or architect, by technical adviser or theatre expert. A study at elementary level is necessary, then, not just because it may provide all the beginner need know, but because it also provides the basis of what every expert ought to know.

For the moment, though, let us return to the idea of modifying the stage of the proscenium theatre to suit more modest

ELIZABETHAN PUBLIC PLAYHOUSE
Act One, scene five, of Shakespeare's *Romeo and Juliet*, showing the simultaneous use of thrust stage and centre stage.

scenic demands. This has been done very frequently, and its general failure needs explanation. The idea contains the seeds of its own undoing. A smaller stage volume makes the theatre much cheaper to build. Since it is the scenic world that is being diminished, the proscenium opening will be diminished. Roughly speaking, the narrower the opening the less scenery required. Thus, either the spread of audience is reduced and the back rows pushed farther from the stage, or the capacity becomes so small as to be uneconomical, or finally side portions of seating give so bad a view of the stage that spectators will be dissatisfied. However, usually a narrow proscenium opening is associated with a narrow auditorium, since it is economical to contain both within a single narrow rectangular plan. But a narrow proscenium opening belongs only in a tiny theatre and this fact is usually ignored, with unhappy results. We have been using general terms and not precise measurements. Unfortunately this must be so, since in the end, value judgements wind up the issues; what is too far from the stage for one person may be close enough for another. But the points I am making are valid in general.

Another criticism of a modified proscenium theatre applies to numerous actual examples. The demand to build on the cheap also results in modifications to the auditorium structure. There are in England thousands of small theatres, attached to civic buildings, colleges, and schools that do not allow the audience to see the actors properly, simply because the auditorium floor is flat. There may be good reasons for having a flat floor in most rooms, and we shall pursue some of them when we look at multi-purpose halls and adaptable theatres, but, for all normal purposes, to put the audience in a theatre on a flat floor is to destroy utterly the possibilities of drama. In schools where drama is often forced to endure these destructive conditions, other common errors are committed: money is wasted on putting a series of bars over the stage in imitation of Renaissance scenic techniques: stage lighting is put on such bars in memorial of the time when gas had to be fed through pipes: drab curtains are hung to commemorate classical wings and borders; and money is wasted on elaborate and irrelevant control boards to enable a so-called technician to vary the degrees of badness with which the actors are lit. Now it is true that a stepped or sloping auditorium floor will cost extra money, but to cut out the overhead pulleys and bars will be an economy: free standing scenery is a much better proposition for most schools. Electricity enables us to put spotlights in various places in front of the stage where they can easily be got at without ladders and without winching bars up and down. A small stage can easily be designed to present an immediately available acting area, without the aid of wings and borders: it will begin to resemble an open end stage, but a proscenium opening may be retained if there is good reason for it. If you travel round England looking at the premises where young people must be introduced to drama, the surprising thing is that even five or six per cent of the population retain an interest in drama, after the stultifying effect of so many truly awful buildings. The whole meaning and function of this kind of theatre has been

JAPANESE STAGE

For centuries the Kabuki theatre usually had a form of thrust stage, with long entrance ways which were an important addition to the main acting area. Members of the audience sat in little cubicles, drinking tea.

sacrificed, though a superficial resemblance to the type has been retained. These are imitation theatres. More people go to them than to fully equipped theatres, and form a poor opinion of dramatic entertainment as a result. The whole justification for this kind of building is, apparently, that it resembles a proper theatre. If such buildings are criticized the defence is usually that not enough money was available to do the thing better. But, no matter how glorious the proscenium stage can be at best, is any purpose served by building a disgraceful imitation? Yes, perhaps: it will convince most ordinary, sensible people that the theatre is a waste of time, better spent by audiences in the cinema or in front of the television set, better spent by actors doing a different and more useful job, and a waste of money which, no matter what permissive legislation may allow in the expenditure of rates, will be better not spent at all (a notion that is common all over England).

However, it is true that at the present time, in sharp contrast to the last century, there is difficulty in getting money for building theatres. Surely then it is not enough to knock a few feet off the plans here and there, and the necessity to re-examine theatre design is inescapable. A cheaper form might be discovered or devised, supposing that we do not know one or two already. There comes a point when a good proscenium theatre cannot be achieved with a cut-down budget, and we should know this by now, for two reasons. Firstly, the theatre with an enclosed stage reached a peak at the turn of the century, and many good, solid theatres have been built and are still in use to show us how it is done and how they can be used. During the nineteenth century theatres were built and rebuilt frequently. One of the reasons for this was that they were built of timber, so they often caught fire and were burned down. Experience of theatre building was bought at the cost of many lives. By the turn of the century, fire and safety regulations were thoroughly codified and their efficiency can be judged by the reduction in the number and extent of theatre fires. The period was also one in which good, substantial buildings were the order of the day. These theatres have lasted. Unfortunately this means that we have had little cause to build very much, or to study the nature of the buildings.

Secondly, in Germany, where many theatres were destroyed during World War II, huge sums of money have been invested in theatre buildings, and twentieth-century engineering has been applied to the form, giving us a number of splendid modern examples. German theatres have not been built on the cheap. They are expensive buildings and their quality relates to their price.

During the second world war a number of theatres in England were damaged, but in most cases patching-up put them to rights again, as at Drury Lane or the Queen's Theatre. There has been a growing demand for civic theatres and halls, as well as for school and college theatres. So far these demands have been met, as already noted, inadequately. We have not learned from the example of our own old theatres or of new theatres in Germany. We are, in England at least, a fundamentally conservative nation, and above all in the arts we move very slowly from one idea to the next. It is clear that modern proscenium theatres can be built at a price. The fact that we do not have enough money to build them adequately

ADAPTABLE THEATRES

The drawing (translated freely from a performance of *Die Rauber* at the opening of the Mannheim Theatre) shows a modern adaptable theatre being used with a transverse stage. Although there is a large, well-equipped opera house in the same building, unfortunately this costly little theatre has seldom been used as anything other than a proscenium theatre.

does not deter us from the attempt. We refuse to examine the possibility of an alternative; if alternatives are mentioned we are alarmed. We defend the inadequate thing done on accepted lines, and defy the new idea with whatever argument suits the occasion. Above all, we do not examine the new idea thoroughly, and we certainly will not wish to give it a fair trial or a reasonable test—an attitude that spreads even to the inadequate imitations of our proper theatres, for we are not prepared to examine even these with care: many of the faults in the imitation theatres are literally mistakes that could have been avoided, without affecting cost, if existing knowledge and experience had been used.

As far as the proscenium theatre goes, then, there is an urgent need for us to look at it carefully as a form and to make sure that when money is sufficient full advantage is taken of its potentialities; and if money is short, then it should not be wasted. Technical efficiency is possible after several hundred years of accumulated experience in this form of building, and for this purpose such organizations as the Association of British Theatre Technicians exist. There is very little excuse for technical incompetence. But when money is so short that no proscenium theatre can be properly built, then some other form of theatre must be considered. Unfortunately, we do not have much experience of building other forms of theatre and although it is true that they can, in general, be built more cheaply than proscenium theatres we shall not really know how to build them at all until we have built a few at least on a generous budget with money to spare for a few errors and a few changes of mind. Until we have good examples of these other forms of theatre it will be difficult to appreciate their basic requirements and match up to the demands of economic stringency. We must remember too that a change of form is not in itself a panacea: any form of theatre can be badly built if we are foolish enough to allow it, and the proscenium theatre has no monopoly in this respect.

It would be wrong to suggest that the only reason for building new forms of theatre is that they are cheaper than proscenium theatres. The relative cheapness of new forms is a convincing point when theatres have to be built on the cheap: the money that might build an inadequate enclosed stage is better spent on a satisfactory open stage. However, open stages have their own artistic and aesthetic attractions and we should choose to build them because these attractions appeal to us. It may even happen that the appeal of the open stage becomes so strong that someone will lavish money on its building. This has happened, of course, in America, where new forms of theatre are treated with much the same financial favours as the enclosed stage. There are fine examples of new theatre forms all over America; a thrust stage at Minneapolis, a centre stage at Washington, D.C., and so on. But ironically enough, although these theatres exist, there are fewer theatres of any form in America in relation to the total population or the overall land area than in England. We have a long history to thank for this. The Americans, too often, have to fight hard for any theatre, and it is usually harder for them to get new forms than old. But they are not so influenced as we are, of course, by historical tradition. Nor, in the event, are they quite so cautious in spending money on theatre buildings. If I stress the fact that the open stage is cheaper to build than the enclosed stage it is because we in England demonstrably are not prepared to spend enough on our new theatres with enclosed stages, and because we in England understand money better than we understand aesthetics.

The theatre today is not widely enough enjoyed nor, for the most part, does it give of its best. The theatre is potentially a popular art, yet at present it only entertains a small proportion of the population; more people enjoy watching sport, or staying at home in front of a television set. Perhaps nowadays theatre ought to be an entertainment for a small élite, and I don't want to deny this possibility, though it could still cater both for an élite and for a popular audience, in different theatres. All sorts of theatres can exist side by side. We should have large theatres for popular entertainments, and small ones to cater for special interests: more of this kind than of that: equally, we should have theatres with open stages as well as theatres with enclosed stages.

We have many examples of proscenium theatres and few of other forms of theatre. So I want to present arguments against the proscenium and in favour of other forms, with the intention of encouraging the building of more of them. I am not such a fool as to suppose that what I have to say against the proscenium theatre is all that there is to say; I enjoy working on the enclosed stage far too much not to recognize some of its numerous attractions. But it does seem to have an extensive monopoly which in the end is unfair not only to the new forms of theatre which hardly exist but also to the proscenium theatre, which appears all too often as an inadequate imitation, and to the drama as a whole, which compares, as far as popularity is concerned, unfavourably with other entertainments:

3—(G.502)

notably cinema and television. I believe that if we enlarge the
scope of drama we may increase its significance and popularity.

It is often argued that theatres come after plays, and that
there is no sense in building new forms of theatre until new
forms of play exist for them. In the main this is a partisan
statement in favour of the *status quo*, for very few playwrights

THEATRE IN THE ROUND

The modern stage, like its ancient predecessors, puts a special emphasis
on actors, their costumes, and props.

will be so foolish as to write for theatres that don't exist; thus
we shall not build new forms of theatre until there are plays for
them, and since no-one will write plays for non-existent
theatres we shall never have new forms of theatre. Yes. But
it is not so simple as this. We do have plays that were written
for other forms of theatre, such as the plays of Shakespeare,
which we can assume were written for a thrust stage. Yet we
do not let this stop us from putting them on enclosed stages.
And one might therefore argue that we should be prepared to
stage on a thrust stage plays that were written for the enclosed

stage. Our love of Shakespeare's plays has not notably en-
couraged us to try out the thrust stage for his or any other plays.
And if we investigate the possibility that Shakespeare's plays
may have also been done on a central or a transverse stage, it is
apparently unnecessary to try these out either. Further, the
fact is that new plays have been written for new forms of
theatre, though admittedly few of them. We must surely
conclude that virtually any play worth doing can be done on
any form of stage, sometimes for better, sometimes for worse;
and there are plenty of other elements beside the form of stage
that may determine how good or bad a performance will be:
notably the degree of skill in the actors. To argue that the new
forms of theatre must wait for special plays is simply a gesture
of cowardice in the face of a call to adventure.

The cinema and television have taken over from the theatre
not only the scenic world, but much else besides: actors, plays
and technicians. They have taken over the vocabulary, even
the word "theatre" itself, the equipment and much of the
function of the theatre. But an important difference remains.
Television and cinema present shadows, and the audience is
entertained by a show of action that is controlled and determined elsewhere. Films are made without the presence of an
audience; and even when a television play has a studio
audience, the viewers who form the main audience are not in
the studio. In a theatre, actors and audience meet each other
at the moment of performance, they share the experience and
each contributes something towards it. Real actors, acting in
the presence of a real audience: this is the essence of theatre.
In designing a theatre this meeting can be seized upon and
developed so that the presence of the actor is more strongly
felt and the contribution of the audience is increased.

Although stereoscopic views featured early in the history of
photography, the cinema has not yet perfected three-dimensional entertainment. Television has virtually left the field
untouched so far. To present the audience with a three-
dimensional image is the unique privilege of the theatre. More
can be made of this privilege, particularly if we surrender the
idea of the picture-frame whose primary purpose was to mark
the beginning of the area of illusion, the scenic world, but
which has tended to flatten actors into the bargain.

The case for new forms of theatre must be based on the argument that they are relevant to our own times. In order to put the case fairly we must first admit that the new forms are not all that new. Most of them have historical precedents. I have already pointed out that the proscenium theatre has an ancestry in the Italian Renaissance, and the line has come

THRUST STAGE

The drawing is based on the Festival Theatre at Stratford, Ontario, in Canada. The plays of Shakespeare seem to come particularly alive on this form of stage.

down to our own day without serious break. Open stages may have more distant origins, but their development has been interrupted, and often they have only survived after years of neglect. These progresses are worth examination. We must ask what theatres were like before the Renaissance, and then try to see if other and earlier stages have any validity now. The last half of the question can in part be answered by looking at modern examples, and in part by theoretical reasoning. But a real part of the answer must escape us. It is bound up with a bigger question: why do we have theatres at all? And it is impossible to prepare an answer to this without taking in every aspect of drama and a good deal of literature, philosophy, religion, anthropology, sociology, and psychology. I am certainly not qualified to conduct such an inquiry. But we cannot avoid the fact that almost any social activity, such as theatre building, reflects in little the whole state of society. We get the theatres we deserve.

We get the theatres we deserve. This suggests that we can interpret many aspects of past times by a careful examination of theatre plans. Indeed, if we also examine what remains by way of records about acting, if we read and perform plays of earlier times, if we trace back entertainment and ritual to their beginnings, we get a fair view of history. In this view the names of battles and kings may be few, but man's relationship with god and the universe, man's dealings with man, and the evolution of society will be exposed clearly enough.

We are mainly concerned with the present. We get the theatres we deserve. If you take a deterministic view, then, there is nothing we can do about it. Here is the theatre, even with all its limitations, as it is because our society is conservative and lazy. There is nothing I can do about it; nor you. But such a view is utterly inappropriate within the realm of the theatre. From its beginnings drama has been concerned with action, it has been driven along by the idea of will; and, faced with disaster or with success, the chief figures of dramatic literature have been manufactured to persuade us that human endeavour, no matter what the opposition, is worthwhile. I am attracted by the idea that possibly some fresh thinking about the theatre may lead to activity within the theatre that will in turn lead to wider, beneficial activity in society. As the theatre reflects society, so does society catch something back from the theatre. The opportunity is there. We can choose to pursue it, or not.

## II

## CENTRE STAGES

THE simplest way of marking the differences between open and enclosed stages is to examine right away the extreme form of open stage, where not only is the acting area in the same room as the audience but it is completely surrounded by the audience. Some people call it an island stage. The first thing to notice is that more audience can be got within a given distance of the stage, by virtue of this complete surround, than with any other form of theatre. Next, it follows that there cannot be any ordinary scenic background; and, though this presents a disadvantage for those who do not like seeing the faces of other members of the audience, it implies the obvious economy that no scenery, scenic spaces, designers, stage hands, and storage rooms normally associated with scenic presentation need be used. Thus a theatre in the round, all things being equal, is likely to be the cheapest form of theatre to build as well as the cheapest to run. Of course, actors will be required to act with their backs, and most critics and other authorities on the theatre will object strongly to the whole idea, thus turning into desperate fanatics those few people who might otherwise have been mildly interested in this interesting form of theatre (Plate I).

It is about the simplest and most complete theatre you can devise, and is a constant taunt to those well-meaning cultural organizations that say they want a theatre, but cannot afford one. Nonsense! What they mean is that they cannot afford a marble monument. A civic theatre, in particular, is looked on as a trump card in the game between rival communities, and there is a belief that provided the front of the theatre is trumpery no other expenditure need be considered. The trumpery, though, is usually so expensive that the same money would have provided several good, solid theatres. A theatre can be built efficiently without great expense, if it is really a theatre we want. Only too often local councillors, and others who find themselves in control of the money available for theatre building, know very little indeed about the theatre. They have memories of glorious pillared façades in front of nineteenth-century theatres and they suppose that monumental architecture is essential to theatres and will alone justify the expenditure of public money.

As far as I know, at the time of writing this, there is in England only one theatre in the round; a converted cinema at Stoke-on-Trent. It is, I hope (having designed it), an interesting theatre, and a creditable achievement in view of the small amount of money spent on it. But for good examples of the central stage, one must look to the United States, where every shape and size in the round can be found. The Arena Theatre in Washington is square in plan and holds 700 people; the Playhouse in Dallas is circular; the Arena Theatre at Tufts College is elliptical and holds 200; the Casa Mañana at Fort Worth is circular and holds 2,000; and so on. Some of these theatres are fully professional, some are semi-professional community theatres, some college theatres for students. The plays presented may be classic or modern, commercial successes or new plays, straight plays or musicals, with large or small casts, and sometimes the lighting and the scenery will be simple and at other times complex. The acoustics of some of these buildings have been designed for central staging while with others the acoustics are a matter of luck since they have been converted from all kinds of other buildings.

The wide range of size and activity can be explained, to some extent, by the fact that the central stage is both the simplest and probably the most common primitive form of theatre. Initially all that need be involved are the two groups of people who are essential to all drama: actors and audience; any space will serve. If what the actors are doing is interesting enough, people will stand round to watch them. If the activity is very interesting, more people will collect, and soon the outer circle of people will not be able to see. There are two solutions to this difficulty. Firstly, the outer rows can be raised step by step so that people in the audience see over the heads in front of them to the acting area in the centre. Secondly, the acting area itself can be raised.

After this starting point, theatre development is likely to take place, to find ways to accommodate the audience as well as possible. Rows of raised levels all round a central acting area demand a good deal of building work, and most sensible people don't like labour of this kind; so it is not surprising that, in the past, when raised levels were built they were merely trimmed out of a convenient hillside. But hillsides do not go round in neat circles. This, among other considerations, leads naturally to the type of theatre associated with ancient Greece, where a circular acting area is partially surrounded by seating. The central stage has become a thrust stage. Similarly, the moment a stage is raised so that a standing audience can see the actors properly (this means a height of about eye-level, say 5 ft. for a standing audience), it becomes uncomfortable to watch from all round because of the masking that takes place; i.e. a distant actor will be hidden by the lower part of a nearer actor, and we will catch a glimpse of the one through the legs of the other. In addition, a raised platform suddenly poses for the actors the problem of getting on and off stage; it is seldom easy to do this effectively climbing steps. So a portion of the platform is curtained off. This gives the actors a tiring room. It also prevents the audience from surrounding the stage. The actors, too, can now overcome the masking problem by, to put it crudely, forming a line across the stage at right angles to the main line of sight from the spectators. We have arrived at the booth stage, and theatre in the round has disappeared.

Actors and audiences are not so categorical about forms of theatre as we have to be in our searches for historical origins and aesthetic justifications. In the middle ages, all kinds of entertainment flourished, from singers and minstrels, to jugglers and acrobats, from mimes to conjurors, from dancers to animal acts; and the occasion might be a market day, an annual festival, a wedding, or a holy day; the place might be the lord's hall, the market place, the open fields, the church; sometimes elaboration was called for, and sometimes the utmost simplicity. Medieval plays made use of all the facilities and techniques of these various entertainments, and of course booth stages were common, and so were central acting areas, and often enough both were used together. The most wonderful of the medieval dramas were the cycles of plays that depicted the bible story from the creation to the last day of judgement, in performances that lasted for several days. The common staging technique seems to have combined booth stages with a central acting area, the stages being arranged round in a circle, leaving a central acting area. The audience could move about freely from stage to stage and also form a circle round the middle which was particularly important as an acting area for vigorous happenings, fights, dances, and journeys on horse-back.

There are several drawings showing the layout of the booth stages or mansions for the Cornish mystery plays, attached to manuscripts of the plays. It is interesting that after hundreds of years in which the plays were handed on by word of mouth, they were eventually written down to meet the demands of Tudor censorship. Unfortunately this censorship aimed at pre-venting the performance of these plays which offered a Catholic view of the world, unacceptable to a new Protestant monarchy. A vigorous and exciting theatre was gradually strangled by red tape and killed off by authority. But it had lasted a long time. The smallness of our store of information about it is due to the thoroughness of the Reformation in burning documents, and to the very popularity of the drama itself: it was taken so for granted, like breathing almost, that nobody considered it strange enough or rare enough to justify the labour of written commentary, until a few people in authority decided to clean up public taste. Then the account was drawn up. A by-product of the misfortune survives in the very valuable record both of the plays and of these particular drawings.

In spite of the staging diagrams attached to medieval manuscripts, there survives very little evidence about the development and forms of Shakespeare's theatre. The scarcity of evidence has caused modern scholars to try and reconstruct in their minds the Elizabethan playhouse, the definitive thing, as though only one type of playhouse could be made out of so little material. Books about Shakespeare's theatre usually tell us that a platform used to be set up in an inn yard, and from such origins the Globe theatre evolved. But the evolution could surely not have been so simple? How could the Eliza-bethans ignore their own bearbaiting pits, which were so nearly ideal theatre structures, and the rounds we have just mentioned, which were already fully fledged theatres? It is sensible to guess that these and many other buildings and conventions

influenced the form and growth of the Elizabethan theatre, and
that in Shakespeare's time, as at most other times (certainly
when the drama is flourishing) there are likely to be several
different forms of theatre, all contributing to the pleasure of
the playgoing public.

The possible relationship between Cornish theatre in the
round and Elizabethan playhouse has been briefly explored by
F. E. Halliday,[1] and the simultaneous use of central and
peripheral acting areas for a production of *Twelfth Night* is
the theme of a book by Leslie Hotson.[2]

A special form of centre stage possibly derives from the
gradual reduction of peripheral mansions to two. By ancestry
they are heaven and hell, but they lend themselves to the
opposing forces that provide the central struggle common to
so much drama, from early times to the present day. This stage
divides the audience into two parts. It can be called a transverse stage. There is evidence that medieval drama in Spain
used the transverse stage in open-air performances. Modern
examples include the Teatro Sant' Erasmo in Milan and the
tiny Traverse Theatre in Edinburgh.

Obviously a transverse stage fits happily into a fairly long and
narrow hall, common in Elizabethan England. Leslie Hotson
has stated a strong case for supposing that a hall or chapel in
the days of Queen Elizabeth I was easily transformed into a
theatre in this way.[3] He describes in detail how King's College
Chapel must have been prepared for a visit of the Queen in
1564. Here the stage was raised, and on one side sat the Queen
with her ladies in waiting and courtiers, while on the other a
few rows of members of the university sat down with the crowd
standing behind them (Fig. 1).

The Elizabethan transverse stage reflects nicely certain
social aspects of theatregoing. To begin with, as suited those
days royalty was isolated on a throne and surrounded by
waiting-women and aristocracy, all of whom were completely
separated from the common people, differentiated in their turn
by sitting or standing, as well as by proximity to stage, of
course, but also by distance from the upper classes. Then

---

[1] F. E. Halliday, *The Legend of the Rood* (Gerald Duckworth, London, 1955).
[2] Leslie Hotson, *The First Night of Twelfth Night* (Rupert Hart-Davis, London, 1954).
[3] Leslie Hotson, *Shakespeare's Wooden O* (Rupert-Hart Davis, London, 1959).

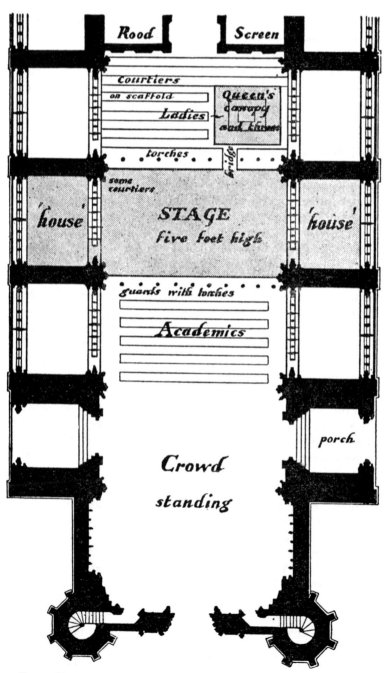

**Rood** | **Screen**

Courtiers
on scaffold
Ladies
Queen's
canopy
and throne

torches · · · · · · *bridge* · ·

some
courtiers

'house'

STAGE
five feet high

'house'

guards with torches · · · · ·

Academics

porch

Crowd

standing

FIG. 1. KING'S COLLEGE CHAPEL, CAMBRIDGE, PREPARED FOR PLAYS, 1564

(*Drawing by Nicholas Wood, from Leslie Hotson's "Shakespeare's Wooden O"*) consider that while the Queen, the ladies and courtiers might really be interested in the play that Cambridge had got ready for the occasion, the residents of Cambridge would almost certainly be more interested in having a good look at the Queen.

The transverse stage itself suggests certain special performance techniques. It invites fencing and fighting, of which the Elizabethans were fond, and also the type of play in which duels were also carried on in words; the opposed mansions must have suited absolutely those historical plays in which two houses fought for the crown, as in the Wars of the Roses, or those domestic conflicts, such as *Romeo and Juliet*, where lovers and their families provided the main elements of conflict.

On a modern transverse stage the acting techniques correspond to those of the centre stage. This is because whichever way the actor turns he has as many people behind him as in front of him; and he must project his performance in every direction. Let us contrast this with acting on all other forms of stage, whether open or enclosed, where a mean line can be imagined between the extreme edges of the audience, and the actor may legitimately project mainly along this line; I call it linear projection as opposed to the organic projection which is demanded by the centre stage and the transverse stage.

If the reformation obliterated the medieval popular theatre, the Commonwealth did nearly as much for the theatre that followed Shakespeare. Buildings were pulled down and performances prohibited. Not much survived to provide the Restoration monarchs and their aristocracy with entertainment, which was therefore imported from Europe, in style if not quite literally. From the Restoration onwards, theatres in England were built in the new Italian style. They were proscenium theatres with enclosed stages. No upheaval has disturbed the development of the enclosed stage, though it suffered the setback of World War I and the arrival of cinema. It continues to dominate our ideas of theatre. However, since World War II, with its destruction of buildings and the resulting re-evaluation of concepts such as permanance and function, new forms of theatre have begun to assert themselves. New theatre forms may be a passing fad, they may replace the established proscenium theatre, or they may, together with enclosed stages, permit us to enjoy a new golden age of drama.

The Reformation and the Commonwealth brought to an end the theatres that provided us with most of the inspiration for our new forms. The gap, however, cannot be depicted quite this precisely. Even in the nineteenth century, when the playhouse had become large and formalized it could in some cases be combined with a circus, as in Astley's Amphitheatre. The entertainment on such stages was hybrid. Animals performed alongside actors. Early in the century, patriotic dramas with equestrian displays were based on contemporary events such as the Battle of Waterloo, or the Battle of Alma. In 1831, Byron's *Mazzeppa* was first presented; it was revived many times, notably with Ada Isaacs Menken in the name part. *Dick Turpin* provided the basis for an ever popular equestrian drama. A later manager at Astley's, William Cooke, cherished the ambition to present all the plays of Shakespeare on horseback. *Macbeth* and *Richard III* were among his successes. For some years Astley's became a formal playhouse, and then finally again a circus and playhouse combined, known as Sanger's Grand National Amphitheatre. It was closed in 1895 when the Westminster Bridge was built.

Modern centre stages arose in Europe as an element in the New Movement in the theatre that exhibited such revolutionary zeal in the 1920's. The prophets of the new movement were Adolphe Appia and Gordon Craig. They were rebelling against both false romanticism and crude realism. Most of the reforms resulting from the Movement were in décor and production. From this period derives the present emphasis on the producer (or the director) in the theatre. But, even if only in a small way, the established form of theatre, with the proscenium arch, came in for criticism. Adolphe Appia and Dalcroze presented Claudel's *The Tidings Brought to Mary* on a central stage at the School of Eurythmics in Hellerau. But such productions were occasional and had little effect. In criticisms of the proscenium theatre, reference was frequently made to the circus, which had an extraordinary appeal to artists and intellectuals as well as to ordinary people, but no theatres with centre stages were built.

The New Movement was never particularly concerned with theatre in the round. It focused its energy, so far as theatre buildings were concerned, on breaking down the conventions of the enclosed stage. Staging reform is often very difficult to follow because of the terms used. If we read an account of an arena production by Eisenstein in revolutionary Russia, it is difficult to be sure whether this used what in our terms would be a thrust stage or a central stage. If we are told that Reinhardt staged *Œdipus Rex* in a circus it is tempting to claim this for the central stage, in spite of the fact that part of the seating was removed to make way for a substantial stage. The famous Grosses Schauspielhaus, made for Reinhardt in a huge circus building, had a vast thrust stage and an enclosed stage. In spite of its curious connections it does not belong to a chapter on centre staging. The first important production on a central stage in modern Europe seems to have been of Gorki's *The Mother* by Okhlopkov at the Realist Theatre in Moscow in 1933. But the Realist Theatre was fully adaptable, and cannot be listed as a theatre in the round.

The centre stage and the open stage in general gained little in Europe from the New Movement, but European ideas produced a different effect in America, and back from America to Europe came the impetus that resulted in the current interest in new theatre forms. The Teatro Sant' Erasmo in Milan (Fig. 2) opened in 1953, the Théâtre en Rond in Paris (Fig. 3) in 1954, and the Library Theatre in Scarborough in 1955. The Pembroke Theatre in Croydon opened in 1959 and it was in fact run by the American, Clement Scott Gilbert. The Victoria Theatre in Stoke started in 1962. This may not be the complete list of European theatres in the round; the Croydon theatre is no longer working; but a number of small-room theatres, part-time theatres and amateur theatres might be found to increase the number. All the same, it is not an impressive total.

Meanwhile, many more examples of theatre in the round can be seen in the United States. Most of the earliest centre-stage productions were presented in schools and universities. Credit for the first is usually given to Azubah Latham who directed *The Mask of Joy* at the Teachers' College of Columbia University in 1914.

Plans for a building specifically meant for theatre in the round were made by Norman Bel Geddes for the Chicago World's Fair in 1922 (Fig. 4); but it was never built. In the

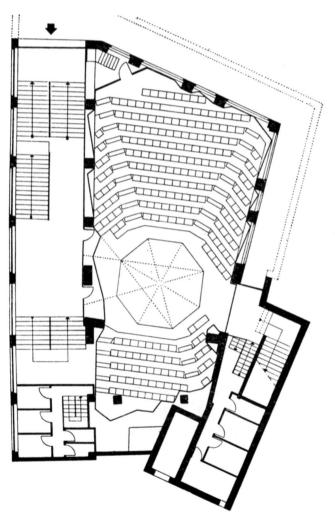

FIG. 2. TEATRO SANT' ERASMO, MILAN
(*Architects, Antonio Carminati and Carlo de Carli*)

31

'twenties and 'thirties, centre stage activity increased, notably at Brigham Young University in Utah, under the direction of T. Earl Pardo; at Pasadena, directed by Gilmor Brown; and from 1932 onwards in Seattle under the direction of Glen Hughes. The first theatre in the round to be built as such was

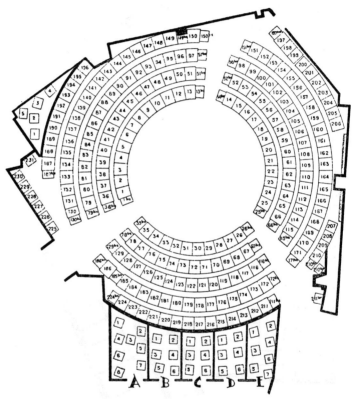

FIG. 3. THÉÂTRE EN ROND, PARIS

the Penthouse Theatre, in the University of Washington at Seattle (Fig. 5); designed for Glen Hughes, it seated 172 people. Although his first production had been *Ghosts* he now found the centre stage most suitable for comedies. It must be noted that this is only one of several theatres on the university campus in Washington. While in England we spend much energy on trying to decide which is the best form of theatre and, since there can be no answer, usually end up with a building

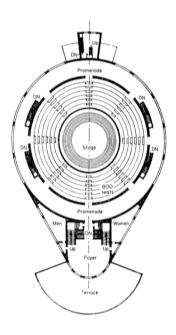

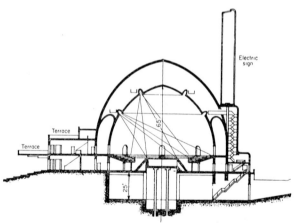

FIG. 4. THEATRE NO. 14
*(Designed by Norman Bel Geddes, 1922)*

that is a compromise satisfying hardly anyone, in America you will usually find that a university has several theatres, each quite different from the other.   Glen Hughes' arena theatre is not spoiled by the demands of, say, a Gilbert and Sullivan group that must have a proscenium arch; instead a proscenium arch is properly provided in another building.   It is not uncommon for a university in America to have four theatres. The result is that each form of theatre has had a reasonable

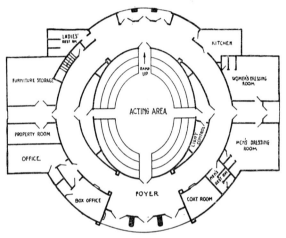

FIG. 5. PENTHOUSE THEATRE, WASHINGTON UNIVERSITY, SEATTLE

chance to assert itself.  And it means that, in this instance, a theatre devoted to comedy does not necessarily declare that the audience is offered a restricted menu; rather, when all theatres simultaneously present their specialities the audience may select with great discretion.

The first professional company for theatre in the round was formed by Margo Jones in 1947, in Dallas, Texas (Fig. 6). It became famous, partly because several new plays from this theatre transferred to Broadway (where, incidentally, they usually failed); but also because Margo Jones, with a deep understanding and great love of theatre, worked successfully on the proscenium stage as well as in the round and carried the attention of audiences and of critics to whatever enterprise she had in hand.  The Dallas theatre seated 198 people.  Its story has been written down by Margo Jones herself.

Perhaps the most interesting development in American centre stages, is the number of music tents. The first was opened in 1949, by St. John Terrell. Called the Lambertville Music Circus, it was housed in a tent and seated 1,000 people.

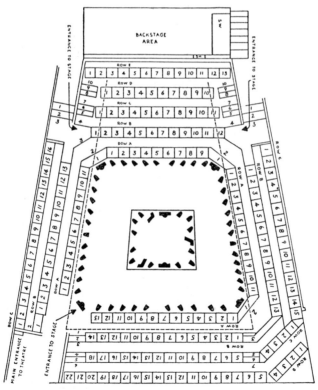

FIG. 6. THEATRE '50, DALLAS, TEXAS (FLOOR AND LIGHT PLAN)
(*Designed by Margo Jones*)

The capacity was later raised to 1,300. There are now many such theatres, usually under canvas, usually operating only in the summer months, concentrating on musical shows, and run successfully for profit.

In twentieth-century England we have a provincial theatre, made up of many long-established companies, presenting plays throughout the year. There are few such companies in the United States, where the provincial theatre has mostly been in the hands of university companies, or community theatres which are mainly amateur. But there is now an increasing tendency to encourage fully professional regional theatres in America. Substantial grants for this purpose have been made by the Ford Foundation, and it cannot be long before government subsidy is given to the same end.

An early example of a fully professional regional theatre, at Houston, Texas, makes use of a centre stage. It has evolved its own presentation techniques, under the direction of Miss Nina Vance. The old theatre was converted from a factory. The stage is square and each side is faced by a more or less square block of tiers for seating. The arrangement may seem open to criticism because each block is separated from the others thus splitting the audience into four separate audiences, and because it by no means gets as much seating round the stage as is possible. But the first objection does not in fact apply in actual performance; each of the seating blocks is roughly the same size and looks much like the others as far as quality of seating and sightlines are concerned: there is no favoured and no inferior block, and this is what can most easily divide and destroy an audience round a centre stage; and the second objection is not important where the theatre caters anyhow for a fairly small audience. The factory conversion has been so successful that the new Alley Theatre is to be built along the same lines. It will seat 300 people. There will, incidentally, be an adjacent theatre, laid out with the auditorium fanning through 90°, seating 800, and with an architectural background (Plates II and III).

In the United States, many examples of theatre in the round can be seen as commercial propositions dispensing light entertainment; as amateur theatre, serving the creative dramatic interests of a community; as university theatre, where the emphasis is more likely to be on the historical importance of the play than on the quality of the performance; and as regional professional theatre, where new plays and classics are presented by a company with high artistic standards. From the many theatres in each of these categories, it is possible to collect a long list of plays and to examine their particular limitations: there seem to be none. The list is comparable, without notable difference, to a list got from other theatres. Of course, a particular playhouse may reflect the tastes of its particular director (as does the Penthouse in Seattle) or its particular policy (as in the music tents); but there do not appear to be any limitations inherent in the form of the theatre.

For a moment, let us look at the all-important matter of acting. I have already drawn attention to the organic projection required on a centre stage, as opposed to the linear projection possible in other forms of theatre. This leads to consideration of acting with your back. Many ordinary theatregoers object to the centre stage because they know that on an enclosed stage actors usually "face front" and that when backs are turned to the audience the actors' impact is diminished. This objection is usually echoed by most experienced actors, and by most critics and authorities on theatre. Now it is true that an actor's back tends to be less expressive than his front (and, above all, his face), and this must be accepted as an important factor in presenting plays in a linear direction. To turn your back on your audience carries implications of bad manners, if not of downright insult. But an actor cannot thus offend anyone in a theatre in the round, for he is always facing his audience; this may sound paradoxical but it can be ascertained by experience. Further, in most cases, the actor does not lose his expressiveness because most members of the audience are so near the centre stage that a whole new range of expression is available to him. His intentions are clear even through his back. Further, few plays demand that an actor should be on stage alone, speaking, for very long; in most plays there is at least one other person to help egg on the drama. Thus the audience may usually expect to get at least one face. At times the reactions of one character will illuminate the intentions of another. Such playing is valued on any stage, but it is particularly useful on the centre stage. It even gives a special responsibility to those confidants, usually considered such dreary parts, in French classical tragedy. Action and reaction, the free use of the whole acting area for the actors to create three-dimensional images, this is the beginning of organic projection. In the end it is not the same as acting for linear projection, and anyone is entitled to prefer one to the other, but there can be no real objection to either. There is, however, plenty of room for personal taste.

What about the scenic artist? It is true that there is no great use for stocks of canvas scenery on a centre stage. But whatever is on the stage should bear the impression of a good artist. And it is interesting to notice that the great American scenic artist, Robert Edmond Jones, could say: " . . . the best thing that could happen to our theatre at this moment would be for playwrights and actors and directors to be handed a bare stage on which no scenery could be placed, and then told that they must write and act and direct for this stage. In no time at all we should have the most exciting theatre in the world."[1]

And Norman Bel Geddes, architect and engineer, gained a brilliant reputation as a scenic and costume designer before he planned his centre stage. Incidentally, I am myself both an advocate of theatre in the round and a scene painter. But Jones and Bel Geddes (and myself) have wide interests in theatre. One can love theatre in the round without having to hate everything else.

The main characteristics of the centre stage can be summarized as follows: it is the most radically different form of theatre, in terms of acting style, from the enclosed stage; it presents the most extreme extent of audience embrace, i.e. the audience is all round the stage: it thus allows the maximum number of people in the audience to be close to the actors; it is the cheapest of all theatre forms; it breaks the greatest number of today's conventions of presentation and thus collects more than its fair share of fanaticism from its supporters and from its detractors; it is as old as the hills (and, in some respects, a good deal older). If you want to explore it, go to the United States (or stay in England and have patience with the Library Theatre at Scarborough and the Victoria Theatre at Stoke-on-Trent).

[1] Robert Edmond Jones, *The Dramatic Imagination* (Theatre Art Books).

# III

## THRUST STAGES

WHILE it is true that the greatest number of people can be got round a centre stage within a given distance, strangely enough a theatre in the round used as a playhouse (i.e. not for musical shows) usually seats only a few hundred people, yet most of the thrust stages we shall now examine seat a thousand or more. Why are theatres with thrust stages so big? I think it is because the thrust stage stretches as far as it will go the spread of the audience while still retaining linear projection for the actor. I believe there is something essentially artificial about linear projection; it provides us with a set of conventions through which we can perceive truth and reality on the stage even when the acting technique is larger than life, grandiose and especially skilful. And I call in evidence the plays that seem particularly apt to the thrust stage: the great Greek tragedies, the plays of Shakespeare, and spectacular productions such as Reinhardt's *Danton's Death* and *The Miracle*, or *Hiawatha* at the Albert Hall, or Peter Shaffer's *The Royal Hunt of the Sun* at Chichester. The emphasis in such plays need not be spectacular; indeed, from a scenic point of view the enclosed stage scores over all your open stages; but spectacle, even if human rather than scenic, there will probably be. Above all, though, the thrust stage seems more emphatically than any other theatre form to invite the richly spoken word. Rich words, gloriously spoken.

But the thrust stage can also function successfully on a small scale. And, in my opinion, as the auditorium begins to come down in capacity to compare with theatre in the round, so the acting style should equally approach more nearly to organic projection. I certainly felt this very strongly when watching plays in Ann Jellicoe's little Cockpit Theatre. This was an altogether exciting venture, the object of which was to explore the possibilities of the thrust stage, set up for each performance in a community centre in Westminster. Plays were given a single performance on Sundays to club members, and about

ten productions were presented before the demands of other
work made Miss Jellicoe give up the enterprise. But a very
wide range of plays was offered, from Aristophanes' *The Frogs*
to John Whiting's *Saint's Day*. One of the advantages of the
Sunday club performance is that experienced professional
artists can afford to give their services for the occasion. I recall
one, in which the company was headed by a very experienced
and talented actress and also included a very inexperienced
and tentative young man; on the small stage her technique
seemed out of place and a performance that really was highly
skilled, in this instance embarrassed many of us in the audience,
while the young man who, amongst other gaucheries, forgot his
lines, didn't know his upstage foot, stumbled on the steps, and
gabbled his words, had such translucent sincerity that we
forgave him his faults and keenly followed the fortune of the
character he so clumsily portrayed. I may be pointing to
differences between large and small theatres, but also to the
fact that the technique of the experienced artist belonged to a
stage that properly benefits from linear projection while the
very lack of such a technique, and in this case of any technique,
helped the young man to stumble toward an organic projection
that was convincingly appropriate on a tiny thrust stage.
However, linear projection is still possible even on a small
thrust stage and, however inappropriate it may be, it is what
actors and critics recognize as "acting."

In England not only has there been considerable confusion
over the terminology of the open stage, which makes discussion
very difficult, but there has also been much misguided activity.
Many people have assumed that once you have an open stage,
of no matter what kind, all linear projection becomes impossible
and what an actor must do to entertain his audience is to
gyrate like a whirling dervish. Such performances have given
the open stage a bad name. The actor on the thrust stage can
use most of the conventions of linear projection familiar from
the enclosed stage, but his vocabulary can be increased, as it
were, with many of the new (and, alas, not thoroughly under-
stood) conventions of organic projection.

In twentieth-century England, a good deal of exploration of
the thrust stage has been done by John English with his touring
Arena Theatre company. The company started in Birmingham

where the seating tiers from an old circus provided the stimulus
to design a travelling playhouse, just after World War II. The
company performed in places where there would otherwise be
little in the way of drama. Thus John English's work never
received the critical appreciation it deserved. But thanks to
his company, many ordinary theatregoers were given genuine
pleasure. And a number of artists have gained insight into
the great possibilities of the thrust stage.

John English arrived at his Arena Theatre (Fig. 7) from a
consideration of the general state of the theatre. He argued
that the theatre of our day had become a minority entertainment, and that we should do something to improve on this.
The decline of the theatre was due to failure to understand that
radio, film and television had all affected the drama, and that
our concept of the playhouse needed bringing up to date.
Obviously to revise the playhouse alone would be of little use.
After 1956 English noted that the Royal Court and Theatre
Workshop had done valuable work with playwrights; but this
work had perforce been carried out in nineteenth-century
playhouses which had blunted the effect of the plays. He
concluded that radical rethinking and replanning were
necessary to find a valid theatre form, which would match the
fresh work of writers, actors, and directors.

The reasoning behind the design of the Arena Theatre ran
as follows: actors and audience come together to share an
occasion. Each group has a contribution to make, so they must
be put under a single roof, in the same room; they come
together to concentrate on the drama to be recreated, and the
drama will therefore be placed in the centre of the room. The
drama needs enveloping, not only by the real world repre-
sented by the audience, but also by the imagined theatrical
world, the scenic background. We thus arrive at a circular
acting area with an audience round three-quarters of it, a
thrust stage. And, because of his insistence on the importance
of the scenic world, John English devised a curtain to wrap
round the stage.

In practice, John English's Arena Theatre had to face all the
problems that beset a new venture launched with enthusiasm
and too little money. But it won audiences, and it was exciting
for actors and directors to work in. It gradually found a style

of its own, characterized by a directness and clarity in interpretation, by visual freshness, simplicity and vigour, and by vocal and physical assurance in the actors. Here was a playhouse

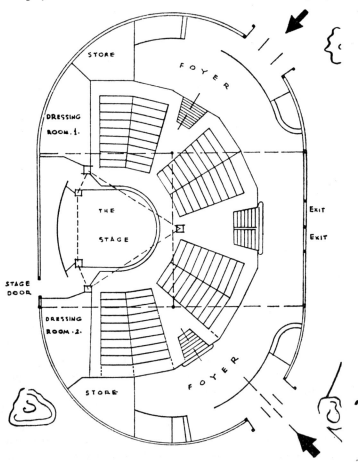

FIG. 7. JOHN ENGLISH'S ARENA THEATRE

that gave everyone an inescapable sense of belonging to the occasion, a playhouse that could take a very wide range of drama and where actors could be at the same time more subtle and more "theatrical." No mean achievement. However, one cannot help wondering if the venture would have received more support from authorities, and grant-giving bodies, as well as from audiences, if it had depended a bit more on the name of Shakespeare, and a little less on a modern concept of theatre.

It must again be admitted that a full understanding of this form of theatre involves a journey to see the Festival Theatre in Stratford, Ontario (Plate IV and Fig. 8), and the Tyrone

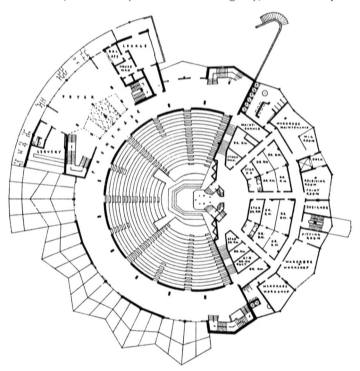

FIG. 8. FESTIVAL THEATRE, STRATFORD, ONTARIO

Guthrie Theatre in Minnesota. These ventures have been given financial backing commensurate with the nature of their enterprise. Even in America money does not come easily to float any hare-brained scheme. But any sensible scheme, even for a new form of theatre, stands a chance; and if the scheme is potentially viable as a business proposition, new artistic ideas will not necessarily be a disqualification. They may even be an asset. The buildings, the first tent at Stratford and the final structure in Minneapolis, have been substantial; the technicians, administration, and artists have been as good as the intentions of the theatres; and there was a harmony of artistic ambition and the means to carry it out made possible by seriousness of purpose on the directorial board, and a theatrical climate tolerant of enterprise if not universally enthusiastic. The ventures have paid off and, as theatres, stand now amongst the most important in the world. To achieve such well deserved success, Sir Tyrone Guthrie, the director of these theatres, left England, where he was already acknowledged to be our greatest director, and went to work in America. In England, as the examples of the theatre in the round at Stoke and the Arena theatre both show, the climate of opinion is unsympathetic if not actively hostile. A board of directors can hardly be found to take such ventures seriously, and, if found, the board will be hamstrung by lack of money, resulting in poor buildings, inadequate staff and administration, and by prospects so gloomy that only a blind enthusiast could carry on. The thrust stage at Chichester managed to materialize and earn fame, thanks to the persistence of Leslie Evershed-Martin, whose brain-child it was, and of Sir Laurence Olivier, who directed the first seasons. But neither of them knew very well what he was doing, and when the building opened it suffered from bad sightlines, bad acoustics, and inadequate technical facilities, while the first plays directed there proved to be awful examples of open-stage production, full of meaningless gyration, restless movement and irrelevant trickery. But, for England, to get this form of theatre up and going at all must be conceded a major achievement. To manage better, Guthrie perforce went to America. And, to see the thrust stage reasonably built and used, we must follow his example.

The Chichester Festival Theatre (Fig. 9) was opened in 1962 with a company of well-known and experienced actors, directed by Sir Laurence Olivier. Since then, summer seasons of plays have been presented. Concerts, recitals and other activities have taken place here at other times. The site is a good one, in a park with many fine trees, and there is plenty of room for cars and buses, which bring the audience from far and near. The building itself is interesting; in plan it is a hexagon. The main roof is nearly flat, though the centre slopes more steeply than the rest. The roof span is 119 ft., and it is supported on a cradle of steel rods and cables, all of which are visible

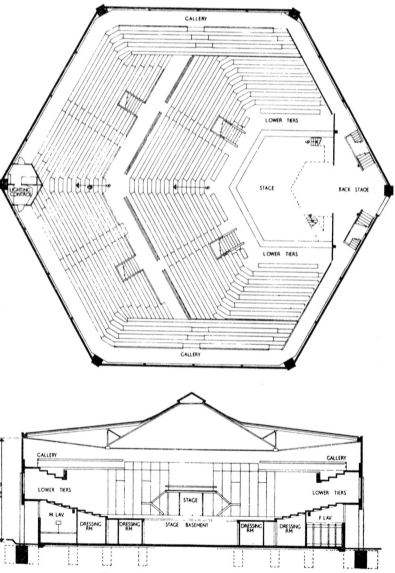

FIG. 9. FESTIVAL THEATRE, CHICHESTER

(*Architects: Powell & Moya*)

45

from the auditorium. The cradle is held at each of the six corners of the reinforced concrete shell which forms the building. The main entrance to the theatre is under a canopy formed by the overhang of the back rows of the auditorium. The stage is at one apex of the hexagon, and the auditorium is arranged to face the remaining four sides of the hexagonal stage. It is slightly raised, and a surrounding step brings it down to the level of the auditorium floor. At the back of the stage, an architectural structure allows a balcony to be erected when required, or various alternative levels, or a special scenic background as required by a particular production. Entrances to the stage can be made through this background, or from vomitories in the auditorium: informal passage can be made to virtually any part of the auditorium by simply stepping off the stage and there is a balcony surrounding virtually the whole theatre for use by actors, audience or orchestra. The whole auditorium is stepped, and on two sides there are balconies. There are 1,360 seats, none of them more than 60 ft. from the stage (Plate V).

The new Vivian Beaumont Theatre in New York's Lincoln Center has a thrust stage (Plate VI). So have many less famous but numerous theatres belonging to schools, colleges and community groups from the University of Waterloo in Canada, to Perth University in Australia, from Bradfield College in England, to Ashland in Oregon.

These theatres vary in size, but mostly they are fairly large, seating more than 1,000 people. The stage is sometimes slightly raised: say about a foot; sometimes as much as 3 ft. 6 in. In plan the shapes of stages and auditoriums may be circular, rectangular, hexagonal, or what you will; and the extent to which the audience wraps round the acting area varies almost as widely. Some have been built to keep pace with modern ideas, others to recapture the conditions and the spirit of the Elizabethan or the Greek theatre.

Finally we are fortunate that a number of ancient theatres with archetypal thrust stages still exist for us to inspect and even to use. It is important to realize that the thrust stage has a very long history and a very widespread distribution, even if we only look briefly in the direction of a few examples.

The simplest form of thrust stage exists without benefit of a complete theatre building. It is no more than a platform, curtained off at the back, to raise the actors so that the audience may see them the better (Plate VII). Such a platform may be made of planks laid on trestles, or consist of a cart or two. The curtaining at the back serves the purpose of providing a retiring space for the actors, and at the same time may enclose a players' room and define entrances onto the stage: as such, it is usually called a booth stage. It is easy to erect, easy to travel, and provides actors with all the necessary means for performing before large audiences. It is not surprising then that the booth stage can be traced to ancient Greece and medieval Europe and may be found in almost any era in China, Japan, India, and wherever unsophisticated theatre still appeals to people.

The classical Greek theatre presents us with a thrust stage that is by no means simple. Its origins remain unknown to us. The ruins that can be seen in Greece are of fairly late Hellenistic theatres, and they have usually been altered by Roman or more recent hands. We are not sure what sort of theatre existed at the time of Aeschylus, let alone in the important period of growth that must have preceded his day. This caution is worth underlining, so that we do not make the mistake of supposing that if the ruins were straightforwardly repaired we should have before us the theatre that provided a platform for so many great plays, and of concluding from this that we should then have arrived at the most successful form of thrust stage. In this connection size is important. Because the ruins at Athens, Epidauros and Megalopolis might seat 16,000 spectators, it has been argued, mistakenly, that we need only build such huge theatres today in order to bring about the rebirth of a great drama. The common assumption is that the great Greek tragedies were written for these theatres. But there is no proof whatever, and very little indication of even the vaguest sort, that Aeschylus or any of the other great Greek playwrights wrote for such huge theatres. An audience of 16,000 would see little, hear little, understand little of a play. And no sensible playwright would contemplate writing for it for a moment. By all means bring on the elephants and throw Christians to the lions (later on). There is good reason to suppose that Greek theatres at the time of Aeschylus were of

various sorts and sizes, but none of them as big as this. It is
very much a matter of opinion how big an auditorium should
be for the staging of plays. But two or three thousand people
seated round a Greek dancing circle looks to me a big enough
audience. Such a theatre might be expected to flourish. Only
one fate awaits a theatre for 16,000: to become a ruin very
swiftly.

In the centre of the orchestra the Greeks usually had an
altar. At the back of the orchestra, a proscenium and skene
formed an architectural background to the action; but how
much action took place on the proscenium (which was a raised
platform) and to what extent the skene was used scenically we
do not know. At the time of the great tragic writers these
elements of theatre were probably built of wood; stone
theatres followed in the Hellenistic period.

The Romans adapted the Greek theatre, making it precisely
semicircular and building the entire structure of stone. Ruins
of their theatres can be seen from St. Albans to Constantinople;
some are in good enough shape, or have been restored, so that
they can still be put to use, as at Orange or Verona.

During the fifteenth century, theatres were built on the
Roman and Greek model as interpreted by Vitruvius in his *De
Architectura*, and the Teatro Olimpico remains to bear witness
of this influence, though it can hardly be said to have a thrust
stage following classical Roman practice. The orchestra has
virtually been abandoned as a performing area, and all the
action at the Teatro Olimpico took place on the stage. Most
of the interest in this theatre, certainly for us nowadays, lies in
the forced perspective vistas behind the openings in the scena.
So much for an academic attempt to reconstruct a theatre of a
past age. It is easy, even for scholars, to miss the point.

Indeed, although much of the impetus behind Renaissance
theatre building came from attempts to recreate ancient Greek
and Roman structures, what came forth in the end was the
enclosed stage with moving scenery. I have commented on
this at greater length elsewhere.[1] Early proscenium theatres
need not concern us here.

But the thrust stage had a wide public in Europe. In Spain,
during the whole period when drama flourished in its golden

[1] Stephen Joseph (editor), *Actor and Architect* (Manchester University Press, 1964).

age, at the time of Calderón and Lope de Vega, the public
theatre usually consisted of a platform stage, thrust into a
courtyard in the open air. The liveliest years of the commedia
dell' arte depended on the booth stage. Our own Elizabethan
playhouse seems to have been dominated by the thrust stage,
and the contracts for the Fortune and the Hope, together
with the famous de Witt drawing of the Swan, and all sorts of
written comments, give us some idea of what the theatres of
Shakespeare's day may have been like.

It would be pleasant to be able to give a full description of
Shakespeare's theatre, or in particular, the Globe, but it is not
possible to do so because we do not have adequate information.
There is always a good deal of specialized research going on
into the matter, and two excellent books by C. Walter Hodges
take the facts as far as they will go.[1] On the other hand we
have a good deal of information that suggests there was no one
ideal Elizabethan theatre; that there were many forms of
stage available to Shakespeare, and that even those theatres
that certainly had thrust stages were by no means all alike. In
plan the Hope was probably polygonal or circular, while the
Fortune and the Globe of 1614 were rectangular. The Hope
had a removable stage (so that the theatre could be used for
such sports as bear-baiting), and if there was a roof over the
stage it was probably not supported on pillars, while the Globe
probably had a permanent stage with a substantial roof over it
that was supported by pillars. Perhaps we ought not to
consider the Hope, since it is virtually an adaptable theatre;
and there is some evidence that many of the playhouses made
free use of the whole arena area for acting purposes, so that
they should really be considered as central stages.

In the nineteenth century attempts to stage plays by Shakespeare under the conditions of his own time kept the idea of the
thrust stage alive: from Benjamin Webster, who tried to
reconstruct Shakespeare's stage for a production of *The Taming
of the Shrew* in 1844, to the presentations of William Poel at the
St. George's Hall. In 1927 Robert Atkins presented plays at
the boxing ring in Blackfriars.

In 1962 Sir Tyrone Guthrie presented *The Three Estates* at the

---

[1] C. Walter Hodges, *The Globe Restored* (Ernest Benn, London, 1953); *Shakespeare's Theatre* (Oxford University Press, London, 1964).

Assembly Hall in Edinburgh. In turning the hall into a theatre
with a thrust stage, many obstacles had to be overcome. A
notable feature of the resulting stage was that the extent of its
forward thrust exceeded its width. Bernard Miles erected a
thrust stage in the Royal Exchange for presenting *Macbeth*,
during the Festival of Britain, and here the stage was much
wider than deep. I think it follows that Guthrie has continued
to explore the thrust stage, while Miles has abandoned it. In
1952 Ann Jellicoe started her Cockpit Theatre Club. And,
more sustained than these ventures, John English has run his
Arena Theatre, set up under canvas or in such a room as the
public swimming baths at Newcastle-upon-Tyne, or in the
grounds of Cardiff Castle, or on the front at Weston-super-
Mare, or in Cannon Hill Park, Birmingham. Bradfield's
Greek theatre was built so that the boys could present Greek
plays in Greek; and, among schools exploring the possibilities
of the thrust stage for Shakespeare's plays, the work of Ronald
Watkins at Harrow is well known.

So many different stages will offer us many different plays.
I have seen *A Moon for the Misbegotten* presented on a thrust
stage in a small theatre in Boston, and *The Way of the World* at
the Tyrone Guthrie Theatre: *Uncle Vanya* at Chichester, *The
Swan* at the little (and short-lived) Cockpit Theatre in London:
a Victorian sentimental drama on the thrust stage of the Arena
Theatre in Newcastle, a medieval mystery play on a cart in
York. You may collect a Greek tragedy at Bradfield, a
Shakespeare play at Ashland in Oregon, a modern verse drama
at the Assembly Hall in Edinburgh, and a further rich variety
of presentations if you travel eastwards to India and China.
As with the centre stage, this form of theatre seems to impose
no special limitations of choice of play.

Sir Tyrone Guthrie presents the case for the thrust stage
at Minneapolis under four headings.

"First, our intended programme is of a classical nature, and
we believe that the classics are better suited to an open stage
than to a proscenium one. Second, the aim of our performances
is not to create an illusion, but to present a ritual of sufficient
interest to hold the attention of, even to delight, an adult
audience. Third, an auditorium grouped *around* a stage rather

than placed in front of a stage enables a larger number of people to be closer to the actors. Fourth, in an age when movies and TV are offering dramatic entertainment from breakfast to supper, from cradle to grave, it seems important to stress the *difference* between their offering and ours. Theirs is two-dimensional and is viewed upon a rectangular screen. The proscenium is analagous to such a screen by forcing a two-dimensional choreography upon the director. But the open stage is essentially three-dimensional with no resemblance to the rectangular post-card shape which has become the symbol of canned drama."[1]

Sir Tyrone Guthrie's concern with the thrust stage arose primarily from his concern with Shakespeare's plays; having done many productions in various proscenium theatres, he began to realize that scene changes were more or less destructive of a play's momentum, that they could be avoided by having a permanent background structure with all the facilities, such as balcony, windows, stairs, envisaged by Shakespeare, and that the proscenium stage limits the vocabulary of action.

"On the picture-frame stage two of the main considerations that govern grouping are to keep the actors facing the audience and to prevent their masking one another, that is to say, standing between other actors and the audience. The considerations often make the movement and grouping of actors more difficult, and less expressive, than it would be if they were disregarded . . . The architectural form of the theatre does make these considerations important."[2]

Guthrie realized that an Elizabethan stage, jutting into the midst of an audience, would make it impossible for actors to face the entire house, and that they could never completely avoid masking, and, what is important, that Shakespeare himself must have known all this. The disadvantages of masking could be overcome by greater fluidity in movement and by the use of raised levels for a figure that must momentarily command

---

[1] Tyrone Guthrie, "A Director's View of the Stage" in *Design Quarterly 58* (Walker Art Center, Minneapolis, Minnesota, 1963). The issue was devoted to the Tyrone Guthrie Theatre.
[2] Tyrone Guthrie, *A Life in the Theatre* (London, Hamish Hamilton, 1960). This quotation is used by permission of McGraw-Hill, Book Company, publishers of the original edition.

the audience's attention over the heads of other actors; and
the disadvantages of having actors who cannot all the time face
front could be compensated for by the fact that when the
audience sits round a thrust stage more people can be accom-
modated near the actors.

The size of auditorium at Minneapolis, or in the Festival
Theatre at Stratford, calls to mind the Greek theatre every bit
as much as the Elizabethan. And there is no reason why the
thrust stage should not be again used as it was by the Greeks.
This must have been the inspiration behind the plans for the
Ypsilanti Theatre in Michigan which will seat 1,900 in an
acceptably classical plan. It is proposed to use wagons for
bringing substantial scenic units on to the stage, and in this
respect the theatre will be essentially modern.

Other examples from America will show how variously the
thrust stage can be used. The Olathe High School Theatre, in
Salina, Texas (Plate VIII and Fig. 10), forms part of a lecture-
room block and can itself be easily used either for drama or for
lectures. In plan the theatre is an elongated hexagon: it has a
large, slightly raised stage and seating for 265. Towards the back
of the stage an isolated wall gives a surface for projected scenic
effects, and the projector is housed in a canopy-ceiling over the
stage area. The canopy also houses a circular curtain track so
that a central portion of the stage can be curtained off; and it
makes a kind of fascia round the stage area, helping to focus
attention there. The architects, Shaver and Company, worked
with James Hull Miller, the theatre consultant, who has made
a special study of thrust stages and projected scenery. Another
modest thrust stage, with seating in three blocks on its three sides
(reminiscent of the arrangement for the centre stage of the
Alley Theatre in Houston, Texas), has been devised for the
conversion of an old building in Cincinatti, Ohio (Fig. 11);
the Theatre in the Park has seats for 227 people in a very simple
plan. A theatre seating 300 people round a thrust stage at the
Darrow School in New Lebanon, N.Y., may be taken as an
example of what can be achieved if a minimal budget is
devoted to a modest and well conceived scheme. Apparently
both school and local community enjoy using the theatre; it
has a friendly atmosphere in spite of its severe finishes—there
was not even enough money for seats on the concrete tiers, but,

I suspect, the plan gives a strong hint of the charm of this little theatre.

What does the thrust stage offer an actor in particular? An actor wants to feel important; he is the more vigorous partner

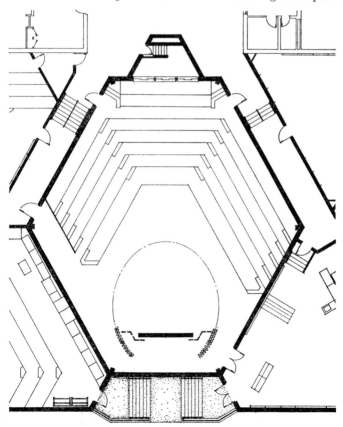

FIG. 10. OLATHE HIGH SCHOOL THEATRE, KANSAS
(*Architects, Shaver & Co.; Consultant, James Hull Miller*)

in the affair between actors and audiences. A raised stage helps him by putting him in a dominant position. He likes to play before many people, and to feel their response to his acting. So he wants as many people as possible near to him. A large number of people in the audience will demand a larger-than-life performance from him: this, too, he enjoys. But if he is to hold the stage alone, if he is to address the audience

directly, then he does not want people all the way round him;
they may embrace him, but he also wants to embrace them, to
take them in swiftly with a single look or gesture. If he is to
take them in thus, he needs a properly distributed audience

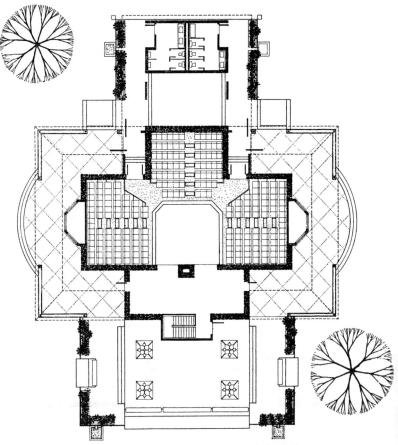

FIG. 11. THEATRE IN THE PARK, CINCINNATI (PLAN)

and if most of them are straight in front of him he will play to
them (as he would on an end stage or even from behind a
proscenium) ignoring the few at either side. An actor who
enjoys this relationship with his audience is likely to find that
certain sorts of play give him the most appropriate words and
actions. This is guesswork to some extent, for we have not

much experience to go on; but clearly the poetry of Shakespeare's theatre admirably suits this stage and the actors on it,
partly because of the language with its magnificent images, its
soliloquies and purple patches; partly because of the rapidity
with which the action is pursued, the swift changes of scene,
the vigorous interplay of dynamic characters; partly because
of the key in which these plays are written, by no means
realistic but concentrated, enlarged and splendid. Further,
this is a stage where the actor can move with great freedom, yet
where certain conventions of movement can be easily established: the advance to centre, the peripheral walk, the action
upstage with the commentator right forward to one side, and
so on.

Among artists who have described the pleasure of acting on
a thrust stage, Margaret Rawlings, defining the fan-shaped
auditorium with the spectator's eyes coming from the actor's
left and sweeping through to his right, quotes Clemence Dane's
lines:

> Oh, I faced
> The peacock of the world, the arch of eyes
> That watched me love a god, the eyes, eyes, eyes,
> That watched me die of love.

This vivid outcry comes from the play *Will Shakespeare* where
the character, Mary Fitton, (replacing a boy actor) has just
been on stage to play the part of Juliet. To think of the theatre
with a thrust stage as the peacock of the world is delightfully
histrionic and evocative.

Finally, then this is a stage where the actor can swiftly play
on the feelings of his audience and himself feel them strongly
before stirring them up to a climax: it is, in other words, a
stage where great tragedy and great comedy can flourish.
What more can an actor ask?

These remarks have, of course, been coloured by the inescapable thought that Shakespeare's theatre had a thrust stage. I
make no apology for this; and it seems to me that plays less terrific than his tend to look a bit thin when presented on a thrust
stage—at least in a large theatre. No play looks thinner than a
verse play written by someone who supposes that literary skill
is the only skill required by the dramatist. Great prose works
approach more nearly the essential poetry of the theatre, and

Chekov, Ibsen, Strindberg come near to meeting the challenge of the thrust stage in this respect. Romantic plays, such as Rostand's *Cyrano de Bergerac* (presented at the Stratford Festival Theatre) are likely to succeed while drawing-room comedy will be more difficult, though this is the kind of opinion that may look very silly in the light of experience yet to come. Of present-day playwrights, Arden will probably be a better bet than Pinter and, in general, large-scale works may be more at home than thrillers with a small group of suspects.

The audience in a theatre with a thrust stage will expect to enjoy the privileges proper to every theatre; that is to say, the right to see and hear properly. In addition, if the thrust stage is to make any sense at all, there must be no feeling that the seats at either side are not so good as those centrally placed. Because of the nature of the entertainment likely to be presented here, the theatre should give the audience a feeling of grandness. Comfort and colour will be helpful. The Tyrone Guthrie Theatre makes a particularly exciting impact on the audience as they come into the theatre on account of the variously coloured seating; it lends a richness and unexpectedness to the place and begins to create from the start a self-interest in the audience, a shared pleasure, that will soon turn them into one responsive being when the play begins. An audience round a thrust stage must, like all audiences, undergo a transformation into a single being, but they should also be aware of their size and power and grandeur.

The theatres with thrust stages that I have seen have all been limited in scope by considerations of expenditure. But one way or another, each architect has contributed to the desired effect. At Chichester one is impressed by the simplicity of the external form, by the glass adjacent to the stairways that deepens in colour by degrees as one enters the auditorium, and by the colour of carpeting and upholstery in the auditorium itself. At Minneapolis, in addition to the coloured seating, there is an impressively layered ceiling suspended like a giant piece of sculpture, and the daring asymmetry of the whole place which is yet clearly centred on the stage; the colours on the stage and overhead muted, dark, and one's attention is swiftly thrown onto the comparatively small stage; as the house-lights fade one's last impression is of a mass of people glowing with anticipation:

then the lights come up on the stage . . . If these theatres have been built on limited budgets, it is still an advantage of the open thrust stage that by almost any comparison it will be cheaper than a proscenium stage for an equally big audience. The main concern of the architect will be to devise a shape in which the thrust stage can dominate the audience, can take a commanding place within a volume that handles sympathetically the actors' voices, and provide the stage lighting upon which a modern theatre depends. And the size of the place must always be related to human size, so that both actors and audience feel at once that they belong here, even if they are not exactly at home, as indeed they are not.

Essentially, a thrust stage is a platform set up so that it protrudes into the audience space. It has sometimes been called a three-sided stage because if the platform is rectangular the audience will be facing three of its sides; but thrust stages need not be rectangular, so the term is not always helpful, and it is an ugly one anyhow, which we can afford to drop. All the same, a criterion for ascertaining the right to be called a thrust stage must be the extent of the embrace the audience space makes of the stage space. A good example will give the actor, placed more or less centrally on the stage, a sweep of at least 180° to take in the audience, and the possibility that people will be equally distributed in any section of that sweep. It is not a true thrust stage if most of the audience is immediately in front of the actor, with a few to left and to right of him; indeed such a theatre is usually entirely unsatisfactory since it does not present actors or audience with the opportunities that belong to the thrust stage, nor does it serve adequately as an end stage, and, as far as I know, no special claims have been made on its behalf except in the name of compromise. A thrust stage is usually a raised platform (Greek theatres apart), and the most satisfactory size of auditorium seems to be able to accommodate between one and two thousand people.

# IV

## END STAGES

THE third form of theatre is in several ways the easiest for us to deal with. There are, for a start, several good examples in England for us to visit. As for the artists, the conventions of acting and setting need be no different from those of the proscenium stage. Both audience and actors can understand the end stage without having to make any important alterations to their already familiar ideas of presentation and performance. Yet, to the relief of your councillors and businessmen, it is cheaper to build than a proscenium stage, and has the same economical appeal that is common to all our open stage forms. It really looks as though we are getting the best of both worlds: no deviation in artistic method, and no large demands for money. However, I hope some people will be suspicious of a new theatre form that demands nothing new from any of the people who use it. Of course, though it is possible to pour old wine into this new bottle, it does offer opportunities if we wish to take them, for the exploration of fresh acting techniques, and it can make important use of scenery and scenic background in new and unusual ways.

The three end stages in England are at the Mermaid Theatre, London (Fig. 12), the Phoenix Theatre, Leicester (Fig. 14), and the Hampstead Theatre Club (Fig. 15). Each of these is rectangular in plan, with the stage, a low platform, across one end of the room and seating arranged to face it from raked tiers. They differ in size; the Mermaid seats 499, the Phoenix 275 and the Hampstead Theatre Club 90. I think it fair to say that the middle figure is the most satisfactory; the Hampstead Theatre is too small to be anything more than a club theatre (though this is not to criticize its productions which have usually been excellent), and at the Mermaid, seats in the back rows seem rather far away from the stage. If the Mermaid were wider, five hundred or more people could be brought into the theatre without anyone feeling too far from the stage since the sense of distance depends on the proportion between width and length of the auditorium space, which is more reasonable in the other two theatres.

The Mermaid came into being in a roundabout way. The founder, Bernard Miles, had already tried to reconstruct a Shakespearian stage in two places. Firstly at his home in St. John's Wood, and then in the Royal Exchange during the Festival of Britain. In each case he toyed with a thrust stage,

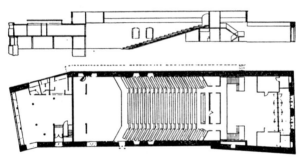

FIG. 12. MERMAID THEATRE, LONDON
(*Architects: Devereux & Davis*)

but in neither case was the audience really distributed round a full 180°; once because the space, being an elongated rectangle, simply couldn't be used for a thrust stage, and on the second occasion, when there was plenty of room, I suspect that caution prevailed and most of the audience accommodation was arranged to face the front of the stage as most people would expect it to. The result of both experiments showed that most people expect to sit in lines facing the front of the stage and not in semicircles round it, and that those few who are silly enough to think otherwise can get a bad view from round the sides of the stage to serve them right. This may be an unkind interpretation of what were, at that time, quite daring adventures. Anyhow, they led to a third Mermaid which had an open-end stage (Plate IX and Fig. 12).

No matter what claims are made for a centre stage or for a thrust stage, the end stage too has its quite specific characteristics, apart from the not unimportant fact, already noted, that no conventional theatregoer need be jolted and no experienced actor need be perturbed. The historical antecedents of the end stage can clearly be found in the many performances in

banqueting halls and inns of court ever since the middle ages.
The Tudor interlude could be taken as a starting point. But
there is no guarantee of continuity here; whenever a platform
has been put up across one end of a hall it has, since the middle
of the seventeenth century, usually tried to become a "proper"
proscenium theatre, an attempt which goes on today in many
schools and colleges and provides them with inadequate
enclosed stages and prevents them being exciting theatres with
end stages. In fact the history of the end stage is a chronicle
of golden opportunities lost. This is the price paid for the
advantage that the end stage has in being so like the proscenium
stage; build an open-end stage, by all means, but then put a
proscenium arch on it, which is easy enough to do, and you
have the snags of both without the advantages of either. It is
the ease with which this disaster can be invited that makes me
so reluctant to commend the end stage at all. However, there
are at least these three good examples of end stages where the
opportunities have been seized, and it is important to account
for them.

In modern theatre history, the first signs of an open end
stage can be traced back to nineteenth-century experiments in
reproducing the conditions of Shakespearean stagecraft on
enclosed stages. Here also began the modern movement
toward the open thrust stage. But put a permanent setting on
to an enclosed stage and you have something like an open end
stage; like enough to suggest that an open end stage is a valid
theatre form. Of course, to blank off an enclosed stage in this
way is both wasteful and not quite successful.

From the beginning of the nineteenth century the idea of a
permanent setting for Shakespeare's plays stimulated German
scholars and directors. Schinkel, Tieck and Immerman all
produced schemes that would enable the plays to be presented
without scene changes. In the middle of the century, Ben
Webster staged *The Taming of the Shrew* in London against
curtains and screens, and later William Poel began his famous
productions that led to a more profound understanding of the
Elizabethan stage. Meanwhile, the predominant mode of
staging during this period grew increasingly spectacular and
realistic. As theatres got bigger and bigger to cope with
increasing spectacle, acting perforce became less and less

"real." A conflict between the delights of visual gluttony and the pleasures of realistic imitation broke out with the attack of Ibsen and the disciples of a literary theatre on the absurdity of melodrama. The battle, as commonly reported, resulted in a victory for the realists. But, not so often noted in this connection, there were full theatres, large theatres, numerous theatres for melodrama, and the literary drama after the conquest could command only decimated audiences, small theatres, and few theatres, which were soon all crying out like spoiled children for subsidy. The key battle itself centred on Ibsen's realistic plays, and it was fought by the French director Antoine with the Théâtre Libre, which was opened in 1887.

Antoine, rebelling against the artificiality of nineteenth-century acting, demanded that the actors should behave as though the fourth wall were there; the stage is, as it were, a room with the fourth wall removed so that the audience can see what is going on. And what is going on must look as nearly as possible like reality. Great attention was paid to setting, furniture and costumes in order to give as real a picture as possible. The Théâtre Libre did not last long, closing in 1896, after severe financial difficulties. But its influence was enormous. It inspired directly such companies as Stanislavsky's Moscow Art Theatre, Otto Brahm's Freie Bühne in Berlin, J. T. Grein's Independent Stage Society (and subsequently therefore virtually the whole provincial repertory theatre movement in England), and even the "little theatre" movement in the United States. It established the realistic style of playwriting, presenting plays by Tolstoy, Strindberg, Hauptmann, Bjornson, Curel, and Brieux, besides Ibsen himself. In England, the realistic movement gave us such new writers as Shaw, Galsworthy and Granville Barker; in Ireland, Synge, Yeats and Lady Gregory.

The literary realists did not have it all their own way. In the name of "literature" they may have banished melodrama; which promptly returned (with music) as opera and ballet. Side by side with the realists and their tendency to explore the sordid aspects of life and to present it in drab colours, the exponents of ballet revelled in brilliant colour, richness and exoticism. Look at Bakst's designs for *Scheherazade*, listen to Stravinsky's *Rite of Spring*, conjure up (if you can) Nijinsky dancing *L'après-midi d'un Faune,* or follow the activities of Diaghilev, who made the *Ballets Russes,* and you may sense some of the lush magnificence that filled the theatres of Europe's capitals in the decade preceding World War I.

Then came a new revolution. This lushness was, equally with drab realism, eschewed by Copeau. In the *Nouvelle Revue Française* of September 1913, Copeau contributed a manifesto in which, while deploring the machinery and material complexity of the stage, he stated his aim of restoring to the theatre its proper splendour, for which the appropriate instrument was a bare platform. This he proceeded to erect in the Old Saint-Germain Athenaeum, which became the Vieux-Colombier (Fig. 13), opened in 1913. It was converted with the minimum expenditure. At first plays were presented against a background of curtains, but in 1918 Copeau and Louis Jouvet devised an elaborate permanent setting of platforms, stairways and balconies which, with a few scenic additions, could form the background for almost any play. This theatre may be counted the real forerunner of our open-end stages. The permanent setting revealed that plays could be presented without tremendous expenditure of time and money on scenic background, and that a good actor can perform to the top of his bent without canvas flats, box sets, or other pictorial paraphernalia. The architectural background was brilliantly conceived and used for a number of fine productions.

The Vieux-Colombier continued to use draw curtains for disclosing the scene and it therefore retained a vestigial proscenium arch (in fact, two of them). A very different stage treatment resulted from the use made by Reinhardt of the Redoutensaal in Vienna. Here an imperial ballroom of the eighteenth century was converted into a small opera house and playhouse, without benefit of proscenium arch or any of the expected separational elements between stage and auditorium. The stage was raised, but the whole theatre was illuminated by crystal chandeliers. A balcony at the back of the stage gave onto sweeping stairways down to the acting area: an architectural background.

The effect of an open stage on actors and audience is incredibly difficult to define yet incredibly powerful. The difference between an enclosed stage and an open stage cannot be measured. You may sometimes sense it when a theatre with an enclosed stage, that has a forestage, is used in such a way that action flows from upstage down on to the forestage: perhaps a single character may move during an important speech, or

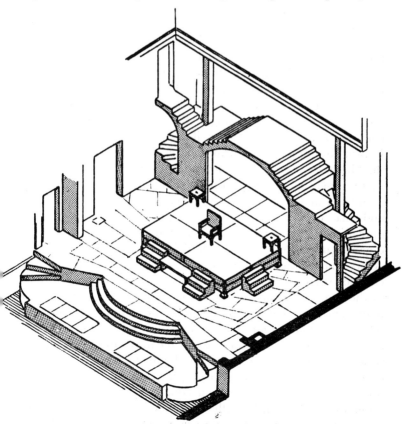

FIG. 13. STAGE OF THE THÉÂTRE DU VIEUX-COLOMBIER
(*Designed by Louis Jouvet*)

scene, from the one to the other. I have noticed such occasions at the Aldwych Theatre (where a forestage has, perhaps inappropriately, been erected for the Royal Shakespeare company's productions). As an actor comes down onto the forestage the acting suddenly assumes a new life, a new compunction, a fresh power to thrill, to engage one's attention. In theatres not designed for forestages the effect is incomplete. It is not shared by all members of the audience because too often action on the forestage cannot be seen at all from the back of circles and galleries. Strangely enough, though this is no place to go into the matter at length, theatre directors are as liable to be casual about sightlines as theatre architects: certainly in England you could support the thesis that only a few privileged people are meant to see and hear a play properly. Such a thesis, though, would not find much support at as good a theatre as Nottingham Playhouse; but even here the actor behind the proscenium is quite a different figure from the actor on the forestage. The word intimacy is often used to describe the special effect of the open stage. It is not a word I like in this context. It implies a domestic, if passionate, relationship while I want to emphasize a theatrical relationship in which there shall be passion indeed but not quite, I think, contact. As I see it, the open stage, by putting actors and audience into one architectural volume, provides proximity between actors and audience over a homogeneous range that includes three-dimensional perception and introduces the possibility of organic projection. Let me explain. Proximity means that actors and audience are close together and, of course, an enclosed stage can have the audience as close as an open stage; so the other elements in my description come into play: the homogeneous range means that while the front row is close, the back row is not too far away. Most proscenium stages present a quite different performance to people in the front rows and to people in the back. An actor may be magnificent to the front, or the middle or the back rows, but seldom to all. A few towering geniuses may give an equal impression to all, or a different but differently brilliant impression to each part of the house. The homogeneous impression depends on a small house. But, of course, even a proscenium theatre can be small. Few of them are. It is a question, as ever, of proportions and intentions. Even the small court theatres of eighteenth-century Europe do not provide an equally good view to all spectators. Indeed they were positively intended for the opposite purpose: to provide one seat and one seat only with a perfect viewpoint.

Equally, an open-stage theatre can be too large as we have already suggested may be the case at the Mermaid and at Chichester. The third element, though, in favour of the open

THE LIBRARY THEATRE, SCARBOROUGH
PLATE I
(*Photo, Walkers Studios*)

NEW ALLEY THEATRE, HOUSTON, TEXAS (IN THE ROUND)
PLATE II

New Alley Theatre, Houston, Texas (Thrust Stage)
PLATE III
(*Architects: Ulrich Franzen & Associates*)

Festival Theatre, Stratford, Ontario
PLATE IV
(Photo, Peter Smith, Stratford, Ontario)

FESTIVAL THEATRE, CHICHESTER (STAGE)
PLATE V
(*Architects, Powell & Moya. By permission of "The Architects' Journal"*)

VIVIAN BEAUMONT THEATRE, LINCOLN CENTER,
PLATE VI
(By permission of Philharmonic Hall Program, William Stuart)

*Les Artistes en Plein Air* (FROM AN OLD LITHOGRAPH)
PLATE VII

OLATHE HIGH SCHOOL THEATRE
PLATE VIII
(*Architects, Shaver & Co. Photo, R. H. "Pat" Hayes*)

MERMAID THEATRE, LONDON
*(Photo, Norman Gold)*
PLATE IX
*(Architects, Devereux & Davis. By permission of "The Architects' Journal")*

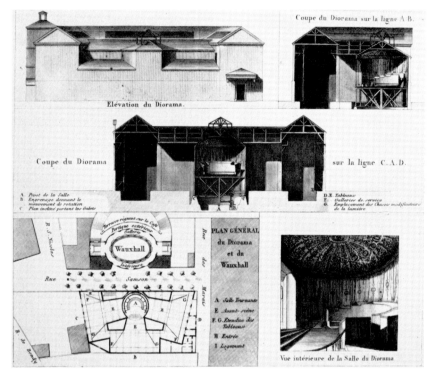

Coupe du Diorama sur la ligne A.B.

Elévation du Diorama.

Coupe du Diorama sur la ligne C.A.D.

A. *Pivot de la Salle*
B. *Engrenage donnant le mouvement de rotation*
C. *Plan incliné portant les Galets*

D.E. *Tableaux*
F. *Galleries de service*
G. *Emplacement des Chassis modificateurs de la lumière*

R. S.t Nicolas

Fournaise régnant sur le Café

Portique extérieur

Gallerie

Intérieure

Wauxhall

Rue des Marais

Rue Samson

R. de Bondy

PLAN GÉNÉRAL
du Diorama
et du
Wauxhall

A *Salle Tournante*
E *Avant-scène*
F. G. *Etendue des Tableaux*
H *Entrée*
I *Logement*

Vue intérieure de la Salle du Diorama

DAGUERRE'S DIORAMA
PLATE X

stage is that the actor can be seen to be a three-dimensional
being, belonging to a three-dimensional world (or even, if you
see the implications, a four-dimensional world). Behind a
frame, on an enclosed stage, even the best of actors is flattened.
On the open stage even the worst of actors will be fully exposed.

As theatre in the round has become increasingly a talking
point, confusion can arise from the literary term, *a character in
the round*. I remember, as a student, discussing the cardboard
characters that one meets in the novels of Dickens; but,
Dickens as well as Tolstoi, has given us characters in the round
too. And even on an enclosed stage we may say of a character,
or of an actor's performance, that it is presented *in the round*.
But I suggest this is a comparative term; bearing in mind how
flat most stage characterizations are, a little extra life and
diversity sends us quickly to a fully-blown-up description.
There is no convenient scale running from *flat* to *in the round*.
No allowance has been made on the way for praise in terms of
partial inflation. And how can a character be more rounded
than round? All the same, the open stage increases our
awareness of the three-dimensional actor beyond the capability
of the enclosed stage, and brings the whole actor/audience
relationship into a new light.

I have already said that a centre stage demands that the
actor should abandon linear projection, which belongs to the
flat presentation of the enclosed stage, in favour of organic
projection. I have also suggested that linear projection can be
retained on a thrust stage and an end stage, and I mean to imply
that organic projection would in each case be better. Organic
projection derives from an acceptance by actors that they are
three-dimensional figures, occupying three-dimensional space;
and it expects the audience to subscribe to this notion. One
would not have thought it difficult to persuade people that
people are really *in the round* and not flat; but experienced
theatregoers and actors have taken it for granted that a
convention of theatre is that people are essentially flat and for
a stage to show otherwise must be somehow impossible, or at
least wrong. Less experienced people should need no violent
persuading. The fact is that actors, like the rest of us, have
backs; and, incidentally, what goes on behind a person's back
may be fascinating to watch. Further, round a centre stage,

6—(G.502)

and to some extent round a thrust stage, another fact is that
people in the audience have faces, and no great harm can come
from acknowledging it. An end stage, though, does not strain
the hardened theatregoer by putting him in a position to see
audience faces. For some very strange reason he needs no
preparation to meet an ocean of heads between him and the
actors.

This attaches too much theory to the Vieux-Colombier,
though the theory might as well be put here since more recent
examples of end stages have tended to plump for the soft option
and behave as though they were indeed proscenium stages.
Interestingly there are few theatres with end stages in America
at the present time. The three present-day examples I have
cited are in England, and I know of none in America in the
shape and form so far taken for granted. But there are many
possible forms of open stage and I may simply be making a
verbal quibble. I admit that what I call *diagonal axis stages* in
certain American theatres are not thrust stages and might, to
some people, seem to be open-end stages. My main reason for
categorizing them separately is that while the theatres with end
stages that I have dealt with are very similar in lay-out to
proscenium theatres, theatres with diagonial axis stages in
America are essentially different from proscenium theatres, both
as far as general lay-out is concerned and in the particular function of scenic and other technical facilities. I interpret this as a
comment on the tendency to treat end stages as makeshift
proscenium stages, acceptable to hard-up Englishmen who are
afraid to make artistic experiments, but meaningless to richer
Americans who at least want something new for their money.

I have made a point of the architectural background at the
Vieux-Colombier. The Mermaid Theatre also has a kind of
architectural background, but it has not been much used. It is
at the back of a fairly deep stage and this decreases its value:
it is too far away from the audience. Besides, there is a revolving
stage in the middle of the acting area and it is this that has
dominated scenic design in the Mermaid. The Phoenix theatre
has also made much use of scenery, and the settings that I have
seen there have been brilliant by any standards. The Hampstead theatre, too, has displayed absolutely conventional
settings for most of its productions as though to say that in spite

of no wing space flats can be displayed as usual. Let us admit that *scenery as usual* remains the motto of these theatres, and perhaps it is unfair to cavil at it; scenery can indeed be one of the attractions of the theatre (Figs 14 and 15).

But what about acting, playwriting, production? The Vieux-Colombier housed not only Copeau's attempts to

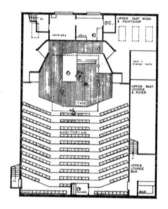

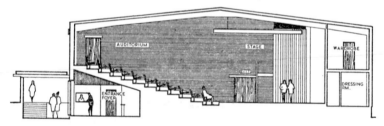

FIG. 14. PHOENIX THEATRE, LEICESTER
*(Architect, City Architect, Leicester)*

nourish an actor's theatre, but also his concern with new plays: plays that escape from the confines of realism and achieved some spiritual significance. Playwrights whose work was staged included Claudel, Duhamel, Romains, Ghéon, Schlumberger, Evreinov, and Gide. But nothing original has come out of our own theatres with end stages except a West-end transfer or two. However exciting productions have been, they have been so in precisely the terms of the enclosed stage.

One other theatre has shown us what might be done even now with an open-end stage. This was the Festival Theatre in

Cambridge (Fig. 16). It opened in 1926 at a time when the producer's theatre had become the fashionable idea. Taken to extremes, as it was at the Festival, this idea was rooted in anti-realism and resulted in such measures as the abolition of properties in addition to the abolition of the proscenium arch. Terence Gray's work at the Festival stands as the best representative of experimental theatre in England between the wars:

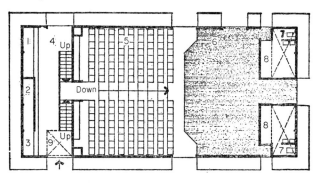

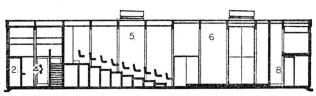

FIG. 15. HAMPSTEAD THEATRE CLUB, LONDON
(*Architects, Ian Fraser & Associates*)

he alone brought to our theatre a completely fresh approach to the whole business of theatre. Open stage apart, he ran, with the theatre, as fine a restaurant as could be found in Cambridge, he invented programmes that could be read in the darkened auditorium, devised new ideas for setting and for lighting, he chose a fantastically wide range of plays, he produced with outrageous originality, and he employed people whose talents soon made them famous: Norman Marshall, Ninette de Valois, Robert Morley, Dennis Arundell, Maurice Evans, Margaret Rawlings, Rodney Millington, and Jessica Tandy to name a few. Norman Marshall has described this important

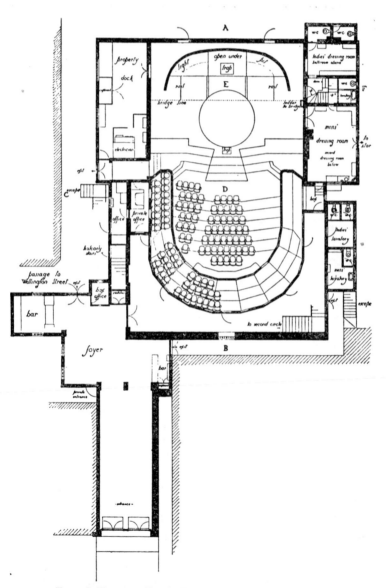

FIG. 16. TERENCE GRAY'S FESTIVAL THEATRE, CAMBRIDGE

venture with understanding;[1] but for the most part the Festival
Theatre was ignored and its influence has been slight, perhaps
because so many of Gray's ideas were so iconoclastic.

From an architectural point of view, the Cambridge Festival
Theatre provides us with a number of interesting features. It
was an old Regency theatre. There could be no escaping the
rough horse-shoe shape of the auditorium, swinging in on two
sides to frame the stage. But Gray virtually removed the
frame, and certainly it was not possible to mark the separating

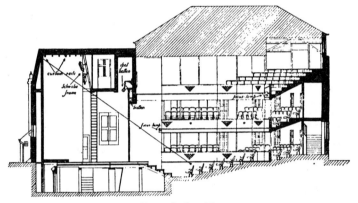

FIG. 16. (contd.)

line between stage and auditorium. A forestage jutted out,
with entrances from what had been side boxes, and steps ran
down into the auditorium; entrances from the back of the
auditorium were much used by actors. A permanent cyclorama
filled the back of the stage and wrapped round its sides. Gray
made considerable use of three-dimensional scenery to provide
different acting levels and to offer various facets to take up
stage lighting. At the end of the Cambridge venture, Gray
planned a new theatre for London but it was obstructed by
current safety regulations and never built; a similar frustration
occurred in Oxford and Gray left the theatre altogether.

In sum, the end stage presents us with an economical form
of theatre, equally suitable for conventional and fresh acting
techniques, able to use ordinary flat scenery, or three-dimensional units on a space stage, or an architectural background.

[1] Norman Marshall, *The Other Theatre* (John Lehmann).

It need offer the audience no surprises at all, though it can be fully experimental.

Incidentally, the word *experimental* has deteriorated and in our present-day theatre tends to mean nothing more than the staging of a new play. The most cautious of provincial repertory companies boasts of an experiment when presenting a new script (in the hope that it will transfer to the West End). By this standard, the commercial managements of the West End have themselves been the most daring proponents of twentieth-century experiment. Sometimes the word is reserved for plays that may incur the ban of the censor, by which device many a dull play has been granted an undeserved success. The word has been cheapened. The activity has been enfeebled. We fall easily into the trap of belittling something important by repeating its name out of context, thus making our lives the poorer; we have done this extensively with so-called four-letter words as well as with words such as *experiment*, which are necessary to describe the processes of bringing life to the arts. It may become necessary even to invent new words. The important work done by the Vieux-Colombier and the Cambridge Festival, called *experimental*, must be carried on by theatres that may have to resort to calling themselves *aggressive, pioneering, way-out,* or whatever best carries implications of assault, onslaught, iconoclasm, radical exploration, and huge entertainment.

# V

## OTHER STAGES

WE have now looked at what seem to be the three main forms of open stage. But there are plenty of other forms, already devised, capable of being devised, and some actually built. Our three categories have been arbitrary, and many theatres will not fit into them. They are not less valid for that reason, and, no matter how untidy our categories will in the end become, there are certain stage forms we must now examine, bridging the gap between enclosed and open stage as well as between the forms of open stage so far acknowledged.

Among the most delightful of theatres, the Georgian playhouses had stages that related in a most interesting and highly sophisticated manner with their auditoriums. These theatres had prosceniums, behind which a full scenic world could be displayed by means of wing space and overhead space. But the forestage jutted out beyond the proscenium arch and formed a complete acting area with the proscenium behind it, the main part of the audience in front, and on either side boxes for more audience as well as doors for entrance to the stage. Strictly speaking these are not thrust stages, but they so nearly serve the purpose as to make us wonder if there is not a direct evolutionary connection between them and the Elizabethan stage.

I have made use of the theatre with a forestage to help define acting style for the end stage, and in doing so may have put the forestage in an unattractive light. To put matters right, let us look at the forestage more attentively. Although it can hardly be called a new form of stage, and is not really a stage at all in its own right (it is only meaningful as an extension of an enclosed stage), it is coming back into fashion along with the new forms of theatre. Examples can be seen at the Belgrade, Coventry, and at the Nottingham Playhouse. A forestage can be defined as an extension to the stage on the auditorium side of the picture frame. It includes the apron stage which is a portable cover that goes over an orchestra pit, as at the Belgrade Theatre.

Most theatres had forestages right into the nineteenth
century. A particularly fine drawing by Sir Christopher Wren,
probably for Drury Lane, shows a forestage extending 17 ft. in
front of the picture frame, and a stage depth behind the frame
of 15 ft. On each side of the forestage there are two doors with
boxes over them. By the end of the seventeenth century one
door on each side of the forestage was the common arrangement. A contemporary etching of the Fitzgiggio riot of 1763
shows that a box for audience has replaced the door farthest
from the proscenium. Prints showing the interior of Drury
Lane in 1775 and in 1808 confirm this. Then there is a
tendency for the forestage to retreat and for the doors to
disappear altogether. The evolution is not precise or straightforward. Wilkinson's *Londina Illustrata* shows, for instance, the
Royal Coburg and the Regency with shallow forestages,
flanked on each side by a single door while the famous print by
Rowlandson and Pugin of the Opera House presents us with a
huge forestage, flanked by five boxes on each side, repeated at
five levels, but no doors at all. George Cruikshank's engraving
that illustrates Grimaldi's farewell performance in 1828 is on a
more modest scale but shows door and box (Fig. 17). This,
with a similar illustration of Elliston and King George II
(Fig. 18), catches a charm that might appeal to audiences in
our own day. At the turn of the century, the stage with a
complete frame and therefore without forestage, became fashionable. When the apron stage can be converted into an orchestra
pit it has usually been without benefit of proscenium doors. In
my opinion a forestage cannot be well used by actors without such
doors or entrances, which should always be provided but often
are not. In modern theatres a forestage can be lowered on
lifts so that when not required it may provide more floor space
at auditorium level, or sink further still to form an orchestra
pit. An excellent example can be seen at the Oxford Playhouse,
where good entrances onto the forestage are provided. At the
Nottingham Playhouse a deep forestage can be obtained by
using lifts in two extensions.

There should be no need to emphasize that a forestage is of
little use unless the actors on it can be properly seen from
every part of the theatre; and that in order to achieve this the
actors must be adequately lit. Unfortunately, a number of

FIG. 17. JOSEPH GRIMALDI, A DRAWING BY GEORGE CRUICKSHANK
SHOWING FORESTAGE WITH DOOR AND BOX

74

FIG. 18. ROBERT WILLIAM ELLISTON, A DRAWING BY GEORGE CRUICK-
SHANK, SHOWING FORESTAGE

proscenium theatres have tried to keep up with the times by building forestages into the auditorium, and not only have these no proscenium doors but actors cannot be seen from circle and gallery; the Royal Shakespeare Company at the Aldwych and the National Theatre Company at the Old Vic have been at fault in this way. In some cases new theatres have been built with forestages but without adequate lighting for them; the Renold Theatre in the College of Technology at Manchester was an example, and, although it must be stated that when plans were first drawn up the theatre had been intended primarily for lectures and only for occasional stage productions by students, all the same it is a bitter comment on the relationship between technology and art that so stupid a mistake should ever have been made at all. Little comfort can be gained from the recognition that this mistake is common, and that the example of the Renold theatre, now partially remedied, has been taken to justify repeating it in other new theatres. Further, it seems to be quite usual for an architect to design a theatre completely and then try to add the lighting apparatus or allow some minor technician to suggest where the lighting should go. All too often a conflict ensues. The useful places for the spotlights will spoil the design, or the lights are inaccessible for maintenance and adjustment. The distress might be avoided if the client specified his lighting requirements, for it is often said that an architect can be no better than his brief. Fair enough. Unfortunately the client often knows as little about stage lighting as the architect, and even when he calls in a lighting expert he may find himself foisted off with a lot of out-of-date and conventional rubbish. There are hundreds of excuses for technical incompetence, and hundreds of examples to prove that technical incompetence is all right. To many Englishmen there is something foreign about technical competence. The Germans put lights in the right places, and the Americans perhaps. But in England artistic endeavour is a privilege of the middle classes and it can only escape the scorn of the upper classes (who may occasionally want to dabble) by being rigorously unpractical. To know how to focus a spotlight belongs to the lower orders, who really could not be consulted when building a theatre. Explain it how you will, few theatres in England have well designed stage lighting

systems. And the worst sufferers are those with unusual forms
of staging, from forestages to, worst of all, centre stages.
Enclosed stages are easier to light, of course, because the techniques were worked out ages ago and all we need do now is to
put these new-fangled spotlights on the same old gas barrels.

It is important that a theatre with a forestage should also
have the facilities to light it, have side entrances so that actors
can use it, and be designed so that people in the audience can
see the action there.

In Chapter VIII I shall make some quite specific suggestions
about sightlines and stage lighting. I have already been
didactic about the acting style appropriate to new forms of
theatre. And I have been as ironical about bringing old-
fashioned acting onto new forms of stage as about out-of-date
attitudes to lighting. But I must admit the dividing line
between acting styles is very difficult to draw, if only because
a good actor is a good actor is a good actor. And stages are for
actors. Theatres are buildings where actors and audiences
meet. The relationship between the two parties may be in-
finitely various, and each variation of stage within theatre
implies a difference in this relationship. Build each form of
theatre well and a whole feast of relationships becomes available,
some of them very special to the palate and exciting to the
playgoer.

Accept, for the moment, that we must devise a theatre that
does all the following things: it allows the actor to perform in
a linear direction, it brings more people near the stage than
an end stage allows, it permits the scenic world to be more
thoroughly exploited than is possible on a thrust stage, yet it
must be fundamentally and thoroughly simple. An interesting
shape and form now offer themselves for your consideration.
The characteristic elements can be seen in the plans for the
theatre Number 6 devised by Norman Bel Geddes (Fig. 19)
and for the Theatre at Western Springs (Fig. 22) for which James
Hull Miller was the consultant. The auditorium wraps round
the stage for about 90 degrees and the angle of viewing is the
same. Richard Leacroft[1] has christened the arrangement a
pictorial open stage, and the aptness of the name lies in its
suggestion of scenic facilities combined with the effect of a

[1] Richard Leacroft, *Actor and Audience* (R.I.B.A. Journal, April and May 1963).

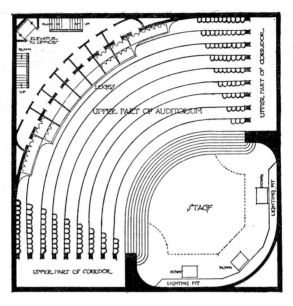

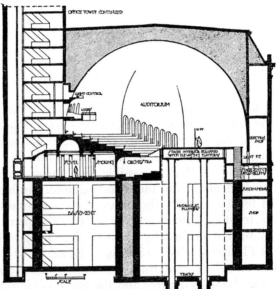

FIG. 19. THEATRE NUMBER 6
(*Design by Norman Bel Geddes*)

one-room theatre, and another name for it is the diagonal axis
stage.

Norman Bel Geddes drew attention to the problem of fitting
a theatre into a typical block in an American city, and suggested
that to plan a theatre on a longitudinal axis, which is the
usual procedure, wastes more space than to design for a diagonal
axis, the alternative he first devised in 1914. The decisive
theatre form that arises when the diagonal axis has been fully
explored need not, in fact, be restricted to the square city lot,
and Bel Geddes developed it in his proposed Repertory
Theatre (Fig. 20), of 1929, which, in plan and in elevation, is
dominated by strong curves. Bel Geddes accepted the principle
that auditorium and stage should both contribute to the
theatrical effect, but he emphasized the scenic world and asked
of the theatre itself that it should be swiftly forgotten once the
scene appeared. The diagonal-axis theatre would use scenery,
free-standing on the stage which, being on an elevator, could
be lowered and replaced by another scenic stage ready to
shunt on to the elevator in the basement. The stage would be
seen when lit, and stage lighting would render unnecessary the
provision of a stage curtain. There would be no proscenium
arch.

The proposed Repertory Theatre formed part of a complex
consisting of a main auditorium seating 1,700, a small auditorium also designed on a diagonal axis, a small proscenium
theatre for children, a cabaret and roof garden, dining room,
dance floor, rehearsal rooms, workshops, offices and all the
ancillary accommodation expected for theatre. It was designed
for the Chicago World Fair to show how drama could be
rationally incorporated in the planning of any large city. It
was an attempt to put theatre in the context of industrial
civilization, on a financially viable basis. A detail, surprising
perhaps in a scheme where economies of space must be considered, is that the back-to-back distance between rows of seats
was planned to be 4 ft. 6 in., audience comfort being considered
an attractive commodity. A more sophisticated design, for the
Divine Comedy Theatre (Fig. 21), makes use of the diagonal
axis principle, but the size of auditorium is so big that a roof of
simple curves could not easily be devised to cover both stage
and auditorium; besides, the stage area has been elaborated to

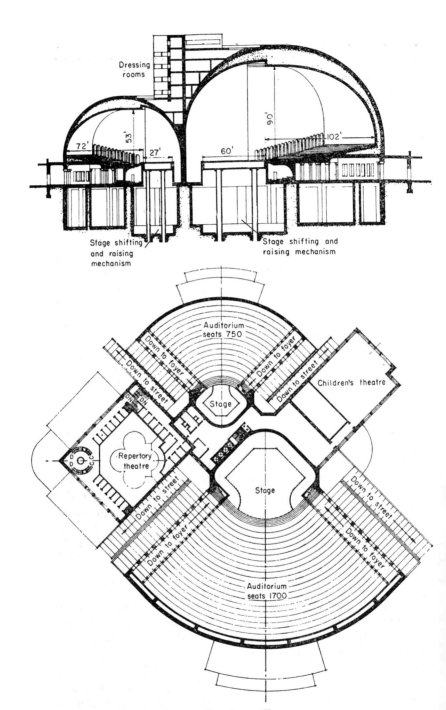

Dressing rooms

53'

9.0'

72'

27'

60'

102'

Stage shifting and raising mechanism

Stage shifting and raising mechanism

Auditorium seats 750

Down to foyer

Down to street

Down to foyer

Down to street

Children's theatre

Repertory theatre

Stage

Down to street

Stage

Down to street

Down to foyer

Down to foyer

Down to street

Auditorium seats 1700

FIG. 20. REPERTORY THEATRE

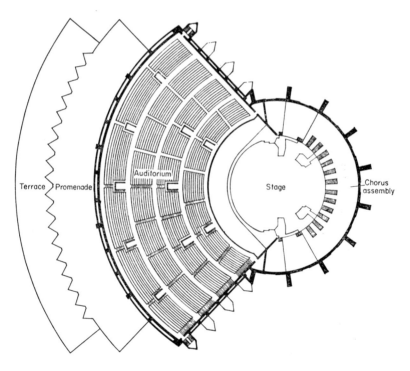

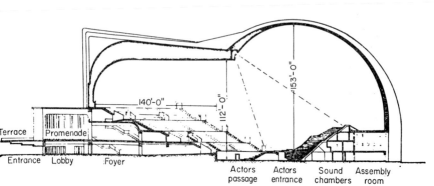

Terrace  Promenade                          Auditorium                          Stage                          Chorus
                                                                                                                assembly

Terrace   Promenade                          140'-0"          112'-0"                    153'-0"

Entrance   Lobby        Foyer                                     Actors      Actors      Sound      Assembly
                                                                  passage     entrance    chambers   room

FIG. 21. DIVINE COMEDY THEATRE
(*Design by Norman Bel Geddes, 1929*)

the point where, though it consists of a permanent architectural setting, it has begun to look like an independent volume, perhaps even an enclosed stage. Indeed Bel Geddes pursued the logic of diagonal-axis design as far as application to a proscenium theatre. His plans for the Ukrainian State Theatre show an auditorium fanned out to 90 degrees facing an enclosed stage, which, though not entirely conventional, allows of full scenic presentation. Again, this theatre was to be part of a complex of several drama spaces and was planned on a grand scale. As a designer of theatres, Bel Geddes showed impatience with the all too common proscenium theatre, and put the case for many different theatre forms. Writing in 1932[1], he said:

"The conventional theatre with its proscenium frame is adaptable only to the peep-show type of theatre. It is a purely two-dimensional medium and seldom used in more than the across-stage dimension. It is not at all suitable for the presentation of such three-dimensional forms of staging as are necessary to obtain correct values from Greek, Elizabethan or Oriental drama, nor for the new, oncoming drama that will develop as a natural consequence of present-day thought and feeling . . . The release of dramatists, directors, actors and audiences from the limitations of the present-day conventional type of theatre would be a tremendous stimulus for the drama."

During the second decade of this century, Bel Geddes began to contribute costume and scenic designs to the theatre; for Reinhardt's production of *The Miracle* in the United States, he converted the Century Theatre into the semblance of a cathedral and made a series of brilliant costume sketches. His set designs for *Joan of Arc*, *Lazarus Laughed* and *The Divine Comedy* have been widely admired. Yet his designs for theatres remained on the drawing board. It is too easy to dismiss his highly original and grandiose theatres as unpractical; but it is true that after quarter of a century or more, they have lost some of their appeal in detail. His new ideas for such mundane objects as weighing machines, gas stoves and bedsteads proved practical enough and contributed to the general progress of industrial design. In theatre architecture, in spite of his deep understanding of theatre and his proven talent, the old form prevailed and this side of his work was ignored. A genius rejected.

[1] Norman Bel Geddes, *Horizons* (Little, Brown and Company; Boston 1932).

In the middle of the twentieth century a number of pictorial open stages were built. They are close enough in comparison with the diagonal-axis stages to justify our looking on them as being in the same category, between end stages and thrust stages, though in America they may be called open end stages. It would be pleasant to suggest that the neglected ideas of Norman Bel Geddes were now, a generation later, finally accepted. This is probably not the case. The pictorial open stages were proposed for a social context quite different from the diagonal-axis theatres, the former being in small theatres for college and community groups, and the latter intended for large industrial city populations. Significantly, the battle was won in the educational field and not in professional theatre. But it was a real battle and each of the new theatres with this form of stage has called for hard campaigning. Probably the most active champion has been the American theatre consultant, James Hull Miller, whose work with the architect, Gus Orth, on the Community Theatre at Western Springs, Illinois (Fig. 22), has resulted in a positive gem of a theatre.

In plan the Western Springs theatre reflects the idea of design along a diagonal axis. The auditorium has seats for 412 and the stage facilities are simple. The seating slope is stepped at an angle of 20° which gives good sightlines to the raised stage and helps to provide good acoustics. Back to back distance between seating rows is 38 in. Stage depth is 29½ ft. and acting area width can be up to 52 ft. The stage is backed by a 32-ft.-wide plaster wall, the entire surface of which is visible from every seat in the theatre. This wall is primarily intended to provide a screen for projected scenery. A low roof covers the entire building, and in the roof (over the auditorium) catwalks have been incorporated so that stage lighting can easily be operated, and a projector is installed in proper relation to the back wall of the stage. The forward edge of the stage can be stepped down into the auditorium or converted into an orchestra pit. Opened in 1961, the Western Springs Theatre has attracted attention from all over the world.

There are several features of theatres for which Hull Miller has been consultant. Firstly, the roof and ceiling line frequently carries on over both auditorium and stage in preference to a raised tower over the stage area. Secondly, stage lighting

facilities are designed integrally with the main structure and
catwalks are incorporated in the ceiling, so that spotlights can
be reached easily.  Thirdly, the seating slope is steep enough to
give good sightlines and acoustics.  Fourthly, the acting area is
wide and in some cases, as at the Senior High School in La

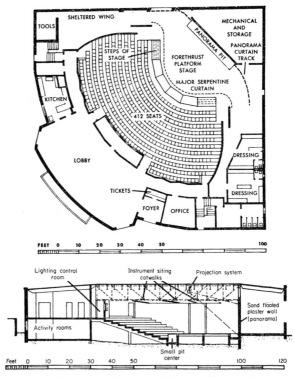

FIG. 22. COMMUNITY THEATRE, WESTERN SPRINGS, ILLINOIS
(Architect, Gus Orth; consultant, James Hull Miller)

Junta, Colorado (Fig. 23), begins to envelop the auditorium;
this envelopment leads to what is called a caliper stage which
offers us the germ for yet another form of theatre.

The stage/auditorium relationship deriving from diagonal
axis planning may appear in many variations.  An interesting
and highly individual example is the Kalita Humphreys
Theatre in Dallas, Texas (Fig. 24), which was designed by the
late Frank Lloyd Wright.  It fairly qualifies as a pictorial open

stage yet has a fly-tower over the stage and therefore a proscenium opening, which is, though, so integrated with the walls of the auditorium as to be scarcely noticeable. It seats just over

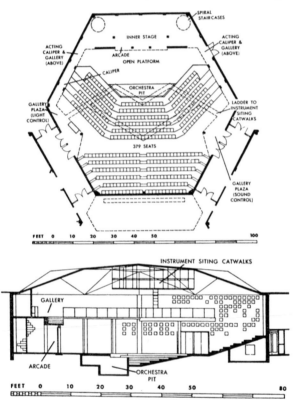

FIG. 23. HIGH SCHOOL THEATRE AT LA JUNTA, COLORADO
(*Architects: Shaver & Company; consultant, James Hull Miller*)

400 people before an acting area 70 ft. wide. The central stage area is dominated by a revolve that has a diameter of 32 ft.

The 90-degree fanning of auditorium with quarter circles of seating on circumferences centred at the back of an acting area suggests an interesting use of a revolving stage. Making use of many features from diagonal axis theatres I have tried to devise a pictorial open stage that might be suitable for a college where stagecraft extends to building scenery, but where the emphasis remains, in performance, on the actor. It is

centred on the revolving stage, and there is no fly tower. The
ceiling over auditorium and stage is trapped so that spotlights
can be manipulated easily, and so that lines can be dropped in
to carry particular suspended items, such as decorative light
fittings, draperies and so on. The intention is that three

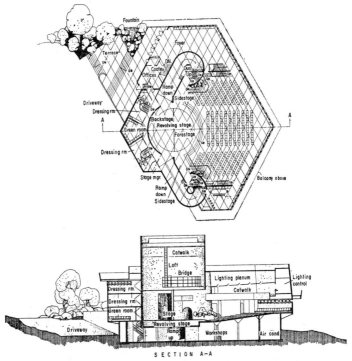

SECTION A-A

FIG. 24. DALLAS CIVIC THEATRE
(Architect, Frank Lloyd Wright)

settings can be built at one time on the revolving stage. A play
may demand more than three sets, and the workshop is placed
so that changes can be made backstage. Alternatively, two or
three different plays may be catered for; and this is important,
for a college may sensibly want the students to spend some time
building a set, and yet have it ready for rehearsals for a week or
more ahead of a performance. Such preparations need not put
the theatre out of action, and performances could still take
place, the stage being turned for rehearsal by day and for
performance in the evening.

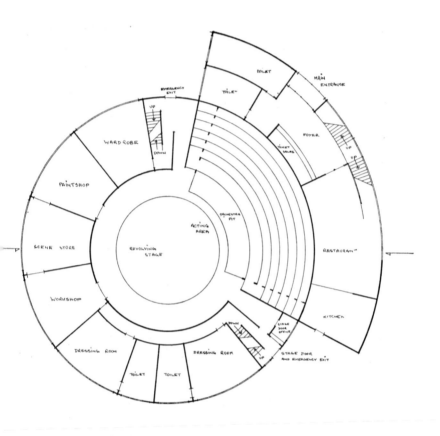

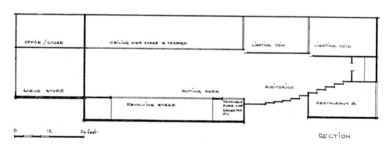

FIG. 25. SUGGESTED THEATRE PLANNED ON A DIAGONAL AXIS AND
USING REVOLVING STAGE

This stage is an attempt to find a positive use of the revolve which is too often misapplied. On an enclosed stage where a safety curtain is installed, the revolve has to be pushed upstage so that awkward gaps appear on either side. Two revolves provide an answer, but at a cost. There is no straightforward solution and the sensible conclusion is not to build a revolve on an enclosed stage at all. If a revolve will help a particular scenic design then it should be brought in as required, size and position determined by the actual demands of the particular theatre and production. The revolving stages at, for instance, the Nottingham Playhouse and the Guildford Yvonne Arnaud theatre offer very limited opportunities. In my opinion, both have been a waste of money and will be a hindrance to many designers. In Germany, however, an answer has been devised in the complete truck stage that contains a revolve to be brought forward when required, as at the Kunstel Theatre where, incidentally, the safety curtain is curved convexly into the auditorium, thus allowing the revolve to protrude beyond the setting line. But this is an expensive theatre, and a quite brilliantly planned one to boot.

You may feel, as I do, that the diagonal axis stage has much to commend it, though scenery apart, it may encourage little that is fresh in artistic approach. Let us turn, then, to a more iconoclastic stage. It is an extreme extension of the caliper stage and owes something to peripheral stages, used in the medieval theatre in the round where the stages were separate scenic units, the audience standing in front of one, then moving to the next as it came into use.

In modern times a mechanized way of moving the audience can be provided by using a large turntable. It will be tipped up to form a wedge, in section (circular in plan). Such open-air theatres as the one at Böhmisch-Krumlau, and another designed by Joan Brehms at Cesky Krumlov, both in Czechoslovakia, make excellent use of this technique. This presents us with an architectural or engineering extreme, but nothing new will be required of the actors. However, imagine the wonderful performance of such a play as *A Midsummer Night's Dream* that could be given in such a theatre, starting in Athens and then, as the auditorium turns, gradually going deeper and deeper into the forest; ending up back in the city for general celebration. Incidentally, the revolving auditorium at Böhmisch-Krumlau is in the grounds of a castle that boasts a beautiful little baroque court theatre in good condition; two such different theatres side by side indicate a healthy appetite, and I suspect the Czechs enjoy their drama a good deal more than we do. They respect the ancient, they revel in the modern. But modern though a revolving auditorium may be, it has interesting historical antecedents, though not quite in connection with the playhouse.

An early theatre with a turntable auditorium was devised for Daguerre's Diorama (Fig. 26). The one in London opened in 1822, had two proscenium openings placed adjacently on the circumference of a circle, inside which the auditorium drum revolved. The front few rows of the audience sat on benches and behind them the majority of the audience stood, while at the back there were boxes. Total capacity about 350. The turntable, ingeniously constructed, could be operated by one man. The Diorama was, of course, not a playhouse and its purely scenic entertainment called for large structures and complex lighting apparatus backstage that could not easily be shifted. And since each picture gave only about twenty minutes entertainment, a longer show had to depend on a movable auditorium. The diorama in Paris had three stages (Plate X).

Another way of moving the audience is for each seat to swivel, like so many executive chairs, as in Charles Laughton's Turnabout Theatre in Los Angeles, where the audience watched either the actors on a proscenium stage, or a puppet stage. In one of the theatres at Baylor University the stage may either be enclosed, with two side stages, or all three stages can be run together to form a complete caliper stage; the main block of seating consists of revolving chairs. Such a theatre will necessarily be small and uneconomical of space.

On the evidence available, it seems that the peripheral stage works best in the open air, with the tilted saucer auditorium, or with a standing audience as in the middle ages. Not many people planning a theatre at present would want to consider a standing audience and for this very reason it is worth saying something in its favour.

First of all, of course, the idea is neither new nor peculiar to

peripheral staging. The medieval theatre of every sort apparently relied on it. We have good reason to suppose that the
groundlings round the thrust stage of the Elizabethan public
playhouse stood. How did they fare? Well, they did not stand

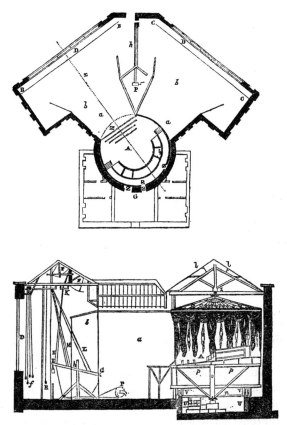

FIG. 26. DAGUERRE'S DIORAMA IN LONDON (TWO STAGES)

still. The main advantage of standing is that you can move
easily to get a better view of the actors, either because they have
shifted from one acting area to another, or because one actor
may be masking another. Sometimes, particularly if the play
is long (as those medieval cycles certainly were), to be able to
move about keeps the blood circulating and prevents cramp;
this may seem a frivolous remark, but even the comfortable

seats of a modern theatre can become unbearable at times, and one reason for having intervals is to give people a chance to move about if they want to. The interval, on this account (and for several other reasons) has nothing whatever to do with acting, with plays or with theatre; it is a part of the price you pay for sitting down. A standing audience needs no intervals unless the actors want one. Another point: we argue a good deal when planning auditorium seating about the back-to-back distance between rows of seats, a minimum distance is required for economy or for packing the audience close to the stage, but more is required for comfortable knee-room for the tall person and for allowing people to pass along a row of seats. Standing eliminates all such argument. It allows people to press close if they wish to, or to move away from the throng. And when there are only a few people in the audience, the actors are not mocked by empty seats. Having said this much, there is no reason to propose standing as a complete alternative to sitting down in a theatre; both might be allowed for. There may always be some elderly or crippled people who want to see the play but who really cannot stand, and I don't want to exclude them, even from my playhouse with peripheral staging.

Another medieval staging technique, apparently common in France and known as *décor simultané*, spread its many mansions and scenes along an elongated platform in front of a standing audience who moved to and fro, like greedy teeth along a cob of corn, as the action went from one place to the next. I do not see much relevance in *décor simultané* to the present day, but it might be useful for staging an industrial pageant or a semi-permanent display of, say, stuffed animals. Before such spectacles, an audience should not be asked to sit down. But I must add that watching many recent productions I have often wished that I were not imprisoned in a seat and could escape without being noticed, as those medieval spectators were able to.

# VI

## ADAPTABLE THEATRES

AN adaptable theatre is one that has facilities for changing from one form of stage to another. It can give you an end stage, a thrust stage, a centre stage, and an enclosed stage; or, if not all of these, a number of variations. The Loeb Theatre at Harvard, the Questors Theatre at Ealing and the L.A.M.D.A. Studio Theatre can each offer at least three different actor/audience relationships.

But before describing a particular example, a paradoxical comment must be made. It is this: for obvious reasons the adaptable theatre is often suggested to meet the needs of different forms of theatre. In a community where an amateur Gilbert and Sullivan society needs a conventional enclosed stage, an experimental group wants a centre stage, and a Shakespeare society would like a thrust stage, an adaptable theatre would seem to be the sensible answer. In fact it is seldom so. Each of these companies has requirements so special that in fact it has, to date, proved beyond human ability to provide for them so as to satisfy each different user. The different stages require differently shaped auditorium plans, they need to be of different sizes, the entrances to stage and auditorium need to be in different positions both in plan and in elevation, and the different levels of stage and auditorium must be in different places. Such a riddle is not easily solved. An adaptable theatre, in settling so many accounts, becomes a form of theatre in its own right. It meets the demands of a director and a company who want adaptability, but not the Gilbert and Sullivan group, the central stagers, nor the neo-Shakespearians.

Theoretically it should be possible to devise an adaptable theatre to please any exponent of each form of stage that is included in its range. Yes, but the expense of doing so would probably be greater than building separate auditoriums and stages for each purpose. A limit has to be put on expenditure, and it puts a practical full stop to our theoretical possibility.

Only the Germans have attempted to spend the necessarily huge sums, and they have failed so far, as in the small theatres at Gelsenkirchen and at Mannheim (Fig. 27). Succeed or fail in this respect, an adaptable theatre is likely to be very expensive

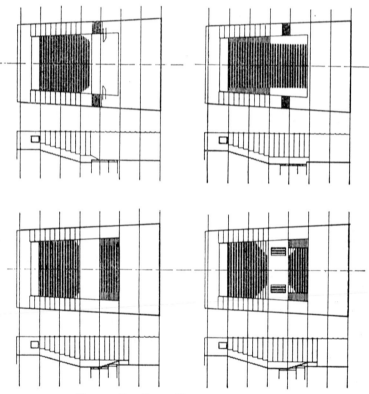

FIG. 27. THE SMALL THEATRE AT MANNHEIM
(Architect, Gerhard Weber)

and the attraction of three forms for the price of one turns out to be misleading: the price will be, more likely, the price of six theatres. An adaptable theatre, as a form in its own right, can only compare in cost with other forms of theatre in the case of a relatively small theatre, such as the ones already mentioned, though the Loeb was expensive by most standards. None of them seats more than 400 people.

Difficulties are there to be overcome. And we have drawn

attention to several that must already add up to a positive
invitation to the ingenious designer. Fine. But a theatre is not
just an exercise in ingenuity; it is a place for actors and
audiences, and ingenuity is only appropriate in their service.
Most adaptable theatres are built to meet the demands of small
communities with an integrated social programme: such as
colleges, as at Harvard: the Questors serves an extremely
enterprising amateur company: the L.A.M.D.A. theatre is a
teaching studio for a drama training school.

The designer of a larger theatre, for more conventional use,
may ask if there is any need to go so wholeheartedly at adaptability? Why not have a conventional enclosed stage, with an
alternative arrangement for, say, a thrust stage? Once again,
the conflicting demands of even two different forms of theatre
are such that either one or both end up so compromised that
the result meets neither: though it may be interesting in its
own right. In a situation where a company wants a thrust
stage, and they are persuaded to play safe by having an
enclosed stage behind it, the result will probably be so poor a
thrust stage that each familiar feature of the enclosed stage
will be seized on to justify the suppression of the other form;
and the final theatre will have an enclosed stage that could
have been a lot better and a lot cheaper if designed this way in
the first place. The tendency to revert to the conventional is
not only a reflection of predominant artistic conservatism, but
it is a simple result of the fact that the enclosed stage is familiar
and we know its pattern and its requirements, while we are less
sure of the essential elements of a thrust stage, and the latter are
therefore more easily sacrificed in design and in practice. In
our example, for several reasons, the company that wanted a
thrust stage will be completely frustrated, and no one else
entirely satisfied.

Perhaps the most satisfactory adaptable theatre is the most
modest. A large room, or studio, with a floor space of about
30 × 40 ft., and a collection of portable rostrums, can swiftly
be transformed from end stage, to thrust and then to centre
stage. It will never make an enclosed stage, unless an adjacent
room is available for the purpose; but then the adjacent room
will spend most of its time as wasted space. The better use of
the adjacent room would be to have an enclosed stage only.

On the other hand, many halls have been built with inadequate enclosed stages and auditoriums with flat floors; and an
improved use for them might be to cut off the stage entirely,
converting it into, perhaps, a dressing room, foyer or workshop,
and setting up in the auditorium whatever form of open stage
might be desired for a particular performance.

A makeshift studio has been concocted on the first floor of
what was originally built as a chapel; it now serves the
department of drama in the University of Manchester. Over
the staircase end of the studio a control room has been built,
with access up a vertical ladder and through a trap door. At
the other end of the studio stands a gallery; the room under-
neath is separated from the rest of the studio by three openings
that can be filled by curtains or by folding panels, and it is used
as a dressing room, or the facade sometimes forms a background
for end staging. The upper level provides storage space, a
raised acting area or an auditorium level as required. All
round the studio, at a height of 16 ft., cable is run in trunking
punctuated at 3 ft. centres by socket outlets. Adjacent to the
trunking, a 2 in. diameter tube bracketed off the wall gives a
means for suspending spotlights. It would have been helpful
to have a walkway all round the room to give access to the
lighting ring, but the poor state of the structure did not permit
this, and access has to be by ladder. Rostrums, stored on the
gallery, can be brought down when required. The studio is
sometimes required with the floor cleared for television work
or for classwork in, for instance, improvisation. To make the
studio as easy to use as possible, the walls are flat and free from
all protrusions; the windows have been completely boarded up:
a handrail on the gallery is removable: the walls have been
painted in dark colours, matt finish; and the floor is covered
with good lino.

A studio theatre with a similar purpose was converted from
a squash court in Woodland Road for the drama department
of Bristol University. It is on a slightly larger scale than the
Manchester studio, and is equipped to provide an enclosed
stage, as well as an Elizabethan thrust stage with a decorative
background. The designer, Richard Southern, has made good
use of the height of the building to provide suspension facilities
for scenic or architectural units.

The new University Theatre in Manchester has what is fundamentally an open-end stage with forestage lifts that are big enough to form a thrust stage. These lifts can sink to make an orchestra pit. And the stage, which is 52 ft. across, can be enclosed by partially opened tab curtains. The theatre is intended to cater for the various drama and opera groups in the university, including the department of drama. It is open to the public, offering, from time to time, performances by professional companies. But good though the general design of this theatre may be, the change from one form of theatre to another involves so many small adjustments that no satisfactory form can easily be achieved. A degree of complication has here been reached so that each theatre form is usually an unsatisfactory compromise when it is presented to an audience: as in the case of most adaptable theatres, it could be better if more pains were taken. But, in the long history of the theatre taking pains has never been a widely distributed characteristic among artists or technicians, and a theatre should surely be designed accordingly.

It seems likely that more universities will build theatres in the near future, and, where there are departments of drama, they will probably be adaptable theatres. The University of Southampton already possesses in the Nuffield Theatre a staging choice between enclosed and thrust stage. The Universities of Hull, Birmingham, and Lancaster are among many with interesting theatre plans. It would be wrong to let the matter go at this, though, because there is still every indication that the problems of adaptability have never yet been adequately solved. One hopes the new university theatres (and others too) will note mistakes already made and avoid these at least; and that where a limited budget imposes restrictions consideration is given to a modest scheme that can be efficiently carried out rather than to a more ambitious building that must be a compromise and remain unfulfilled.

The L.A.M.D.A. theatre was not erected on purpose-built foundations but is the result of knocking two studios into one. A certain amount of permanent structure provides rows for seating, behind which the control rooms are situated. Adaptability is achieved by moving a number of units that form circular tiers: they can all be set out to surround a central stage, or a number of units will give an auditorium for an enclosed stage, or a thrust stage.

An even more ambitious project can be seen at the Questors. It was designed to provide three stages: an enclosed stage (with a variable proscenium opening and optional forestage), a thrust stage, or a centre stage. The basic plan is approximately horse-shoe shaped and this means that part of the seating on each side has to be masked off for an enclosed stage arrangement as sightlines from the sides would be very poor. It also means that the centre stage has one section of auditorium that is makeshift and weak. But this theatre presents us with the only thorough attempt to solve the problems of adaptable staging in this country, and the result is certainly exciting. The architect, Norman Branson, says: "An adaptable theatre of this type had not been successfully designed before because, as G.B.S. said about Christianity, 'it had not been tried and found wanting, it had been found difficult and not tried.' this"

In the United States there have been many adaptable theatres built for universities. The circular structure that houses and gives its name to the Ring Theatre at Miami University is designed so that rectangular and triangular units of seating can be arranged to give a centre stage, a thrust stage (with an Elizabethan-style architectural background) or an enclosed stage with variable forestage.

A highly mechanized theatre, the Loeb (Fig. 28), built for Harvard is based on a simple idea that allows each of the arrangements to look remarkably complete and solid; there is nothing apparently portable or makeshift about it. Essentially, the idea is to have a main level at stage height. Lifts immediately in front of the stage can sink, taking down tiered banks of seating which then marry up with fixed tiers at the back of the auditorium. When the lifts are at stage level the seating on them can be swung on to what was the enclosed stage, thus forming a transverse or central stage; or the seating can be arranged on either side of the lifts which are further raised to form a thrust stage. The enclosed stage at the Loeb is well equipped and the flying system includes George Izenour's remotely controlled synchronous winches. It is an expensive theatre. Incidentally, the building includes a small and

brilliantly equipped studio where experimental forms of open
stage can be employed.

A department of drama in a university where there has been
a long tradition of experimental theatre (this may sound like

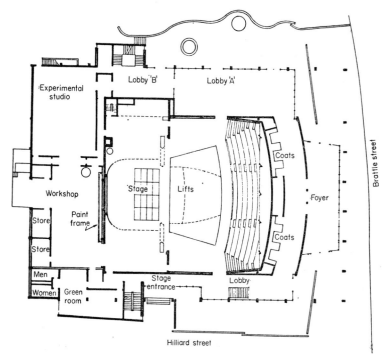

FIG. 28 (a) THE LOEB THEATRE, HARVARD UNIVERSITY GROUND FLOOR
PLAN

a paradox to English ears, if not an absolute impossibility) will
be likely to seek a completely flexible theatre that is virtually
unconcerned with such formal concepts as centre staging or
thrust staging. The University of Texas has a theatre, seating
about 350 people, where walls, floor and ceiling are all adjustable. The floor plan is 60 ft. square, divided into 10 ft. square
units that can be raised or lowered by a special mobile jack in
the basement. The ceiling similarly divided and suspended
from the roof structure, is an egg-crate grid for stage lighting,
and for suspending curtains, scenery or temporary walls.

Among the many schemes proposed for an adaptable theatre, the Totaltheater designed by Walter Gropius has probably had the greatest influence, its main characteristics

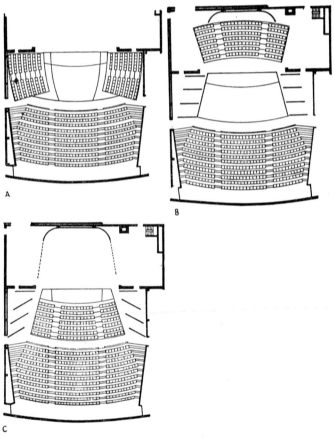

FIG. 28 (*b*) THE LOEB THEATRE, HARVARD UNIVERSITY (ALTERNATIVE ARRANGEMENTS)
(*Architect, Hugh Stubbins & Associates*)

being recognizable in the new Crescent Theatre, Birmingham, and in the plans for Okhlopkov's new theatre. Between the first and the last there is considerable difference in size; but in each of the three examples, as well as in many others, a portion of the auditorium is carried on a revolving platform so that either an enclosed stage or a centre stage can be arrived at.

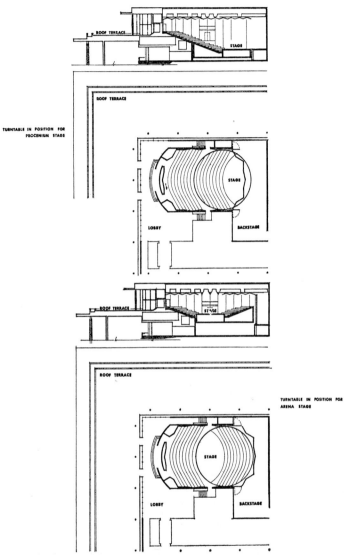

FIG. 29. THE JOHN F. KENNEDY CENTER, WASHINGTON, D.C.
(*Architect, Edward Durrell Stone*)

The John F. Kennedy Center in Washington, D.C. (Fig. 29), has a particularly interesting example (it is one of five theatres planned for this arts complex). Of the 510 seats, about half are on the turntable which, in the centre stage position is jacked up to give a more or less symmetrical section. It is more a transverse than a centre stage. My own view is that the centre stage thus achieved is in no case attractive enough to justify all the expensive machinery required to create it. But there is something very attractive about expensive machinery and probably more people fall for it, and understand it even, than fall for (let alone understand) the theatre itself.

# VII

## MULTIPURPOSE HALLS

A MULTIPURPOSE hall differs from an adaptable theatre in that while the latter is solely concerned with dramatic entertainment the former may also cater for activities not connected with theatres, such as dances, banquets, assemblies and meetings, whist drives, conferences and exhibitions. Indeed many multipurpose halls are primarily intended for such other uses, and drama may be a minor consideration.

When a multipurpose hall is planned, the provision for drama is usually made on an *ad hoc* basis, since no particular user is envisaged. The result is that in most cases a raised stage and a proscenium are built, but not the ancillary spaces backstage without which the enclosed stage can hardly function. Frequently the ceiling level of the hall runs over the stage so that there is actually less height where extra height is most wanted. The actual functioning of the enclosed stage is misunderstood. Access to the stage is often badly placed and inadequate. The backstage area may be cluttered with anything from a water tank to a disposal unit.

But such stages may well be faulted as the result of generous impulses. The stage may have a specially polished hardwood floor, or radiators to keep the actors warm. But the polished floor is a menace to actors and a nuisance when scenery must be set; since it is laid as a feature it must be kept clean and unscratched, a condition incompatible with any practical stage. The radiators are so placed, as a rule, that they get in the way of scenery, or spoil the scenic back wall and, since they must not be covered up, generally restrict the use of already limited areas backstage. Often enough money is spent quite freely on curtains and lighting equipment of which the former are dreary and the latter installed in the wrong places and consists of the wrong instruments anyhow: very few spotlights are placed in the auditorium, and on stage there are battens and floods but not enough spotlights. The spotlights are usually placed where it is difficult to get at them for adjustment.

Another good intention may manifest itself in a plastered back wall representing a cyclorama; but there is not enough depth of stage to light the cyclorama properly and space is so cramped that marks soon appear on the cyclorama from dirty hands, from scenery that has been leant against it and from accidental collisions.

But the main fault with the multipurpose hall, from a theatrical standpoint, is that the floor of the hall is flat and thus, after the first few rows, sightlines are increasingly bad. If the stage is raised to eye-level, which for a seated person can be taken as 3 ft. 8 in. (it certainly ought not to be raised any higher), at the most half a dozen rows may be satisfactory on a flat floor. In a proper theatre the floor would be gently sloped after a row or two, and ideal sightlines from a floor in front of a raised stage are achieved if the floor is sloped at a gradually increasing angle; but for various reasons this is not entirely practicable. A reasonable alternative is to increase the slope once or twice, using steps when the gradient gets beyond 1 in 10 (which is about as steep an incline as feels comfortable, and is the usual limit accepted by authorities concerned with public safety). Note that a uniformly steep auditorium may give unsatisfactory results after half a dozen rows. In a multipurpose hall there are various ways of attaining sloped seating while keeping a flat floor, and since this is so important a matter let us look briefly at some of them.

Portable rostrum units can be employed to raise seating, as at the Technical College in Hemel Hempstead. Pull-out tiers can be built in, as at the Grammar School in Leeds, where these tiers are stored under an extensive balcony which carries on the seating block. A rocking floor can be installed as at the Mitchell Memorial Hall in Hanley. The first of these three methods can be relied on for a rescue operation in a hall already completed with a flat floor: the other two must be planned from the start, and, though they may cost more initially, they make less demands on labour, on external storage space and on maintenance, and they give a more convincing result. However, as we shall see in a moment, portable rostrums have the advantage of permitting adaptable staging by allowing a variety of seating arrangements to be erected. The idea of a rocking floor may sound highly complex, but in

fact Cuvilliés designed one that was incorporated in the
Residenz Theatre in Munich as early as the middle of the
eighteenth century, thus enabling the royal family of Bavaria
to have a flat floor when the theatre served as a ballroom, and
a sloping floor when theatrical performances were given.
Nowadays, the Hall Stage Equipment Company can provide
you with the same facilities, along the same lines but with more
modern working parts (Fig. 30).

The cost of providing, in a multipurpose hall, a floor that
may sometimes be flat and sometimes sloping gives rise to two

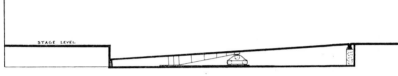

STAGE LEVEL

FIG. 30. TILTING FLOOR (AUDITORIUM) FOR MULTIPURPOSE HALL

other questions. Firstly, is it really necessary to have a flat
floor? An amazing number of activities can in fact take place
in a theatre with a sloping floor, including films, lectures,
conference meetings and demonstrations, and it should be
considered carefully. Secondly, might it not be sensible, in the
long run, to spend a little extra and have two halls, one with a
flat and one with a sloping floor? Even if the argument is put
forward that the two halls will seldom be required for simultaneous use the fact is that each will probably help the other:
certainly a hall adjacent to a theatre offers opportunities for
refreshment space, exhibitions, extra dressing rooms or storage
—all of which are commonly scarce in a multipurpose hall.

So far we have been considering the multipurpose hall that
stretches towards theatre in the direction of an enclosed stage.
It is fair to suggest that such halls might be much better built
than they usually are. But our present concern with new
theatre forms justifies turning to the possibility of using open
stages to serve drama in multipurpose halls.

In a very small hall, an open stage has much to recommend
it. The stage can be kept at main floor level, thus simplifying
the planning of approaches for actors and audience. There is
no need to separate the stage from the hall by any form of

proscenium. An open stage implies a one-room theatre. Open stages do not depend on scenery and they can function fully without it, without curtains and without any technical apparatus that will interfere with other uses. An auditorium can easily be built by erecting portable rostrums and the acting area defined by making use of spotlights. Thus the two positive demands of an open stage on a small multipurpose hall are good storage space for rostrums (and for seating) and good stage lighting facilities. These demands can be efficiently met with very modest expenditure; though of course, if the arrangements are badly planned a lot of money can be spent to little purpose.

Of the forms of theatre we have already mentioned, is any one particularly suitable to the small multipurpose hall? No, I don't think so. If the hall is a long and narrow rectangle (perhaps the cheapest plan to build on), an end stage or transverse stage will probably fit it best. If the hall is more or less square, a centre or diagonal-axis stage will probably fit in well. A medium rectangle will most likely take in a thrust stage. But in the second and third cases a good deal can be said in favour of planning for adaptability and of collecting a stock of rostrums that can be used to define several different forms of theatre. There will probably be little difference in the cost, and, shape of hall apart, choice of theatre form must depend on the interests of local drama groups who may use the hall.

In a larger hall I would still want to consider a fairly modest stock of rostrums so that any form of open stage could be set up when required, but extra money might be spent on good lighting equipment, on ancillary spaces such as dressing rooms, stores and foyer, and on the provision, as part of the main structure of the hall, of a balcony. A balcony could be designed to give an upper acting area, to take a row of seats for audience, or to provide a platform for extra stage lighting; it could give interest and excitement to what otherwise might be bare walls, and it might even have a degree of adaptability so that it could be integrated into a scenic design along the lines of the Vieux-Colombier or, as we suppose, the Elizabethan public playhouse.

A final word of warning here, to anyone involved in planning a multipurpose hall, about walls. If theatre is considered at all, remember that most plays are presented in the evening and make use of stage lighting; the walls should therefore not be made of glass, and the finish on walls and ceilings should, without making the hall depressing, be darkish in colour and non-reflecting (i.e. paint should be matt not gloss). Glass can, of course, be curtained but good curtains are expensive, while cheap ones tend to be only partially efficient and they soon get dirty and are liable to be torn and battered in a multipurpose hall.

In addition of course, daylight is unnecessary during film-shows, banquets, dances, and many other uses to which the multipurpose hall is put. During a daytime film-show an inadequate blackout is a nuisance: for a banquet battered curtains will be a damper of spirits. Therefore the less window space the better. Easily controlled heating and ventilation are necessary for big public rooms: naturally ventilation through open windows is unsatisfactory, particularly in winter. The forced circulation of air, warmed or cooled as required, provides the best answer. But it must operate so that no noise disturbs the theatre. In the United States air-conditioning is common, and theatres benefit. Noisy systems serve as a barrier between the audience and full enjoyment of the play.

# VIII

## SEATING, SIGHTLINES, AND LIGHTING

IF you set out to make a dress, you may be helped by a
pattern, bought for a few pence: or to make a cake, you can
get a recipe; and for many other constructive activities there
are diagrams, formulae and instructions to tell you what to do.
Then what about a building formula for the centre stage, a
recipe for the end stage and a diagram to show you how to
build a thrust stage? This is the kind of help many people
would like and would expect, particularly after the many
abusive remarks I've made about other people's buildings. I
can only disappoint them and admit that the business of
building a theatre is far too complicated, involves far too many
different factors, to be within my grasp. I doubt if even the
liveliest of computers could give the answers that would satisfy
everyone. Strangely enough, the starting point, the main
requirement of a theatre, whether it has an open or enclosed
stage, is simple enough. All you do, as a builder, is to erect a
structure that will enable the audience to see and hear the
actors. The secondary requirements are simple enough, too;
you merely provide some rooms to look after the various needs
of the audience before and after the play, to accommodate the
actors when they are off stage, and to house the various
technicians and administrators who assist the actors and the
audience. It is almost a formula! It certainly possesses one
notable quality of formulae, recipes, and the like: no matter
how accurate it is, you can always go wrong.

A complete recipe apart, the new theatre forms obviously
make only a few special technical demands in detail. But when
planning unusual stages, people often make mistakes that arise
from a misunderstanding of very ordinary procedures. So
there are two kinds of data worth collecting: those which may
be a trifle unexpected, and those which might otherwise be
wrongly calculated. A full treatment of data can be found in
*Theatre Planning* which has been prepared by the Association of
British Theatre Technicians. The Association is continually

reviewing the whole business of theatre planning, and it runs
an advisory service which should be used by the responsible
people for every theatre building, at an early planning stage.
Theatre building is a very complicated affair and, in addition to
the advice of the A.B.T.T., the client or architect should consider
employing a Theatre Consultant. The consultant may be
brought in from the very start to advise on choice of site, form
of theatre, size of theatre, selection of architect even; or he may
be employed by the architect to deal with specific matters of
seating, staging, lighting, or machinery.

In theatres such as the Festival at Chichester, the Mermaid,
the Phoenix and the Traverse, the stage is only slightly raised;
say about 1 ft. A centre stage, as at the Victoria at Stoke, is
usually not raised at all. But most enclosed stages are raised to
eye level of the front spectators, a height of about 3 ft. 6 in.
One wants to raise the stage as high as possible in order to make
the actors visible to as many people as possible, but if the stage
is raised above eye level then sightlines, particularly those of
people near the stage, begin to be cut off. The level of the
stage in relation to the seating levels will control the sightlines.

In working out sightlines, or in checking to see that the
design of a theatre is in this respect satisfactory, certain measurements are worth noting. It is usual to take arbitrary approxi-
mations for these measurements, and I give these, together
with other basic data, at the end of this chapter, on page 120.
If the stage is raised to 3 ft. 6 in. above the auditorium floor
level a few rows of seats may be set out on the floor level.
After two rows the sightlines begin to deteriorate and the
actual number becomes a matter of choice, according to how
poor you will allow the sightlines to be before they must be
improved. In many theatres, sightlines are bad and are known
to be bad, and nobody seems very upset: not even members of
the audience. But I would not recommend you deliberately to
design a theatre with bad sightlines if only because I myself do
complain about them, and I believe that, where people do not
complain, it is either because they are so used to awful theatres
that they don't know sightlines can be good, or because the
entertainment is so awful that it is not worth seeing anyhow.
To build theatres with bad sightlines is common practice, and
is a major factor in determining the relative lack of interest

shown by most people towards drama in England: if you have a puritanical aversion to theatre, or an academic interest in dramatic literature, you may welcome bad sightlines. Then put twenty rows of seats on floor level and most of the audience will not see the action of the play properly (which will help to prove that you get more pleasure from reading a play at home than from going to a theatre to watch it). If you care, as I hope you do, that all members of the audience shall see the play properly, then calculate your sightlines carefully.

A dozen rows can be on a gentle slope of about 1 in 10. From then on the rows should be raised on steps.

We are, at present, dealing with a theatre that has a stage raised to 3 ft. 6 in. If you often go to the cinema you have probably noticed that the main floor of seating has many rows on the level, and then many more on a gentle slope. In some cinemas, the front rows are even on a reverse slope, down from the stage. But remember that in a cinema the screen can be a good deal higher than a stage for actors. The front rows of seats in a cinema are not usually considered the best because of distortions and general lack of smoothness in the picture, so they are cheap; and because they are cheap the extra discomfort of having to look upwards seems to be acceptable. Though if the seats are designed for the purpose, looking upwards need not be uncomfortable in the cinema, and there is, of course no question of cutting off sightlines (the limiting factor in raising a stage).

While we accept that raising each row above the row in front improves sightlines, there are, again, limits to observe. Suppose we simply set each row a foot higher than the one in front, shall we not get perfect results? No. This may be tested at the Bayreuth theatre where, towards the back of the auditorium sightlines are poor. A steady slope loses effect the farther it goes away from the stage. Ideal sightlines involve a gradually increasing slope of the auditorium floor. The principles involved in working out sightlines are perfectly straightforward and only require a drawing board or some mathematical calculation. There are several different procedures arrived at over the ages, and no new factors are introduced by new theatre forms. A carefully designed section, drawn for a theatre planned in 1875 by Davioud and Bourdais, gives us an early example of a floor with increasing slope. The plan for the proposed theatre shows a large forestage as well as an enclosed stage, seating for 9,000 people, and acoustics have

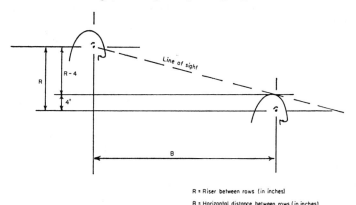

R = Riser between rows (in inches)

B = Horizontal distance between rows (in inches)

DIAGRAM I

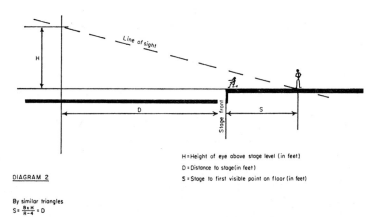

H = Height of eye above stage level (in feet)

D = Distance to stage (in feet)

DIAGRAM 2

S = Stage to first visible point on floor (in feet)

By similar triangles
$$S = \frac{B \times H}{R-4} = D$$

FIG. 31. DIAGRAMS TO ILLUSTRATE SIGHTLINES FORMULA

been as carefully considered as sightlines. Unfortunately, the plan is unattractive.

A practical formula for checking sightlines is given in *Theatre Planning*.[1] It relies on your being ready to lay out your work on a drawing board, and gives you an "ideal" section

[1] *Theatre Planning* (A.B.T.T., London 1964).

from which you can deviate towards a practical compromise. In my own experience, I often find that I want to solve sightline problems when all the instruments available consist of a pencil and the back of an old letter. Further, I don't want to deviate from an ideal but to test a scheme already developed and to know what each person will really have to put up with. And by using a simple formula, derived from the relationships between similar triangles, I can get a useful answer. For what it's worth, here is how the formula works: I want to find, for one position in the auditorium, the nearest point on the stage floor that will be visible to the spectator. In the first diagram, which represents our spectator looking over the head of the person in front of him, $R$ is the riser (or the vertical distance this spectator is raised above the person in front of him) $B$ is the back distance in the horizontal plane between seats. The 4 in. represents the distance commonly accepted as the vertical separation between eye-level and the top of one's head (hats not being normal wear in our theatre). In the second diagram, $H$ is the height of our spectator's eye-level above stage level, $D$ is the horizontal distance of the spectator away from the front edge of the stage, and $S$ (the measurement we wish to discover) the distance away from the front edge of the stage that the spectator will first see the stage. Of course neither of these diagrams need actually be drawn, and I have drawn them now to show the similar triangles and how they give us the formula,

$$\frac{B \times H}{R - 4} - D = S.$$ The measurements derived from the first

diagram should be all in inches, while those from the second are probably better off in feet. This formula works particularly well when dealing with low or unraised stages, and when checking sightlines from distant balconies and galleries.

Remember that an error can creep in to your design if you have a lateral gangway and forget that the slope must allow for it. An example of this mistake can be tested at the Festival Theatre in Chichester. Raising levels of seating is an extra building expense and we want to keep it to a minimum, but don't let motives of economy drive you to accepting low standards: unless, that is, you really want to wreck the theatre.

The desirable seating slope depends on the height to which the stage is raised. If the stage is not raised at all, then the seating rows must be steeply stepped. It is obviously all right to have the front row at floor level. For subsequent rows, if the back to back distance of rows is 3 ft. then the rise should be at least one foot, and preferably more.

I have already given a warning about having too many rows with too steep a slope. If you must raise each row a foot or more, then don't have more than ten rows. Since the only theatre form that positively requires an unraised stage is theatre in the round, and ten rows will accommodate a thousand people or so, this will probably be enough. Personally, I prefer a centre stage with no more than seven or eight rows, which should accommodate about five hundred people. And, incidentally, I like the front row raised: if the slope gives rises of 1 ft. from row to row, the front row should be raised 6 in., which will be the riser of intermediate steps on access gangways.

Between the extremes of an eye-level stage and an unraised stage there are infinite variations, and the many other factors controlling sightlines make it necessary to say that each design should be drawn up and checked carefully. Let us look at some other sightline factors. Back-to-back distance between seats, or rows of seats, may vary between, say, 1 ft 9 in. and 3 ft 6 in. For most ordinary purposes 3 ft may be taken as an optimum distance: less than this will begin to be uncomfortable for tall people, while more will begin to waste space and spread the audience so that they become unsatisfactorily diluted. Note that when seats are on the same level you can put your feet under the seat in front but when rows are raised on tiers there comes a time when this is no longer possible, so a greater distance back to back is required for the latter case than for the former. Also, in the latter case, people passing along rows of seats may feel insecure if there is too little distance between rows since the backs of the lower seats may be too low for them to hold or lean against.

Safety officers in this country usually insist on minimum standards for seating arrangements. Occasionally the standards may be silly and prevent a good design being carried out. More often the minimum standards are sensible. However, minimum standards are, as they claim, minimal; and a well designed theatre will exceed them on the side of generosity. Back-to-back distance between rows of seats is a case in point. Too

many theatres have seating rows closer together than is
comfortable for people who are tall. It is all very well to
defend the distance by reference to an average height, but if
an average means anything at all it includes the essential fact
that some people will be taller than average. Why should they
suffer in the theatre? Further, it may be argued that to make
an audience comfortable is, anyhow, wrong: if the play is
worth seeing, some discomfort can be endured. Yes, but this
thesis has no particular connection with the physical dimensions of members of the audience, and, when designing a
theatre, you should not necessarily assume that tall people will
only come to the good plays while short people patronize the
bad ones in comfort. There may be something to be said for
making expensive seats more comfortable than cheap ones, but
even then the actual space for knee room need not be too
limited, for there are many other ways of making the poor
suffer, be they short poor or tall poor. But if you are a short
person, and want all your spectators very close together, please
note that I have already made a plea for standing room, and I
hope you will take it seriously.

The distance between any two seats in the same row may
also vary. Minimum standards depend on such things as
whether the seats have arms or not. Ordinary stacking chairs
can usually be placed side by side at 18 in. centres, and this is an
uncomfortably small distance for big people. 21 in. might be
an acceptable optimum. Comfort apart, sightlines are affected.
The density of heads will determine the lateral paths of vision.
If seats are set wide apart, it may be possible to stagger the
seats, i.e. set the second row of seats so that each comes behind
a gap in the row in front, and thus avoid some of the raising of
rows we have just been examining. But plot this on paper, and
you will see that staggered seating does little to help sightlines
where the seats must be reasonably close together, where they
are fairly close to the stage, and where the stage is as wide as
most stages are. It may be helpful at the back of a remote
gallery, or if the only object on stage is a stationary figure, or if,
as we started with, the seats are wide apart. Probably more
nonsense is spoken in favour of staggered seats than in connection
with most sightline questions.

Safety authorities usually require that a row of seats is of

9—(G.502)

limited length. However, a longer row may be considered safe if the back to back distance of rows is adequate to provide easy passage way. For enclosed stages there is much to be said in favour of continuous seating, with the gangways at each side of the theatre where sightlines begin to become unsatisfactory; a centre gangway is a waste of good seating space. Besides, it is better to seat the audience in a big mass than to divide them up by gangways into smaller blobs. Continuous rows are called continental seating, chiefly because in Germany, where safety regulations are very severe, most modern theatres use this system.

Don't forget that people often come late to the theatre and it is sensible to provide for them. Latecomers should be let into the theatre so that they can see the performance, but so that they do not disturb the actors or other people in the audience. Avoid bringing latecomers in through doors adjacent to the stage, a mistake made at the Phoenix in Leicester (is it just my impression that certain people in Leicester now enjoy drawing attention to themselves by coming in late?). The worst possible arrangement, exemplified at the Library Theatre in Scarborough, is to have only one entrance for audience and to have actors use the same entrance: latecomers can too easily find themselves following an actor on to the stage. But no-one really designed the Library Theatre; it just happened. Special accommodation for latecomers should be allocated (possibly standing room, again), and access to it should be through doors in double sets that provide a trap to prevent unwanted light and noise from coming into the theatre with them.

In designing an auditorium, I think it important to try and get as many people into as small a space as possible. An auditorium should not have walls: that's good space where people should be. As I see it, much of an actor's power is wasted in travelling over physical distance; and an audience, that singular thing, can only become the single thing that an actor requires if all its molecular individuals are crammed tight and closely related to each other. And, as I have already suggested, I believe this can be done without discomfort; though there is a point where too much comfort will destroy any possibility of an exciting performance. Gangways are a nuisance during performance, however necessary before and

after it, and they should be sited carefully with performance,
as well as escape from it, in mind. Back to walls: mid-century
democratic feeling abhors circles and galleries which it takes
to be the signs of social stratification. Trust mid-century
democracy to worry about removing signs while taking little
trouble to remove the abhorrent thing itself, and to misunder-
stand the signs anyhow! There is no reason why the gallery
should not provide excellent sightlines and be a perfectly good
place from which to see a play, as it was, for instance, in the
Elizabethan public playhouse. Social stratification in Tudor
England must have been more precise than at the present time,
but they arranged their class barriers in the theatre on the
opposite basis from our own. Then artisans and labourers
stood in the pit, and better-off people paid more to get into the
surrounding galleries. There was a good deal of sense in this
method of discrimination. The less educated playgoers got
the full impact of the actor's performance, while the more
refined spectators could sit back and savour the play at a more
comfortable distance. Not that anyone had to be at any great
distance from the stage, the front of which was probably within
forty feet of the farthest member of the audience. Our proscenium theatres manage differently. Their tendency is to have
the smartest seats in the stalls, and the cheapest accommodation
in the farthest reaches of the gallery. Students and working
people get a diluted impression of the play, which may help
account for the fact that they mostly watch television rather
than go to the theatre. The efforts of a Joan Littlewood or an
Arnold Wesker to take drama to the people might be reinforced
by allowing such people to get a good look at the drama for a
change, and subsidies spent on sending out touring units from,
say, the Royal Shakespeare Theatre to factories might be better
spent on putting your factory-hand where he can properly see a
play in the theatre itself. Of course, even in twentieth-century
democratic England, such a procedure might upset the
privileged stallholder. The overall solution that I propose is to
have so few rows of seats that none is too far away, not even in
the galleries; but I suspect the Elizabethan playhouse had a
better answer all the same.

Good use is made of an upper level in both the Festival
Theatre at Stratford, Ontario, and the Tyrone Guthrie Theatre

in Minneapolis. And I think that a good theatre in the round could make use of one or two shallow balconies over the main seating level. In my own particular drawings I have arranged for a standing row behind one circle of seats at each higher level.

Putting the audience on different levels can be achieved in unorthodox ways. At Moline in Illinois, the John Deere auditorium has been designed primarily to exhibit farm machinery, but it can also serve as a cinema. It seats 384 people, facing what is virtually an open end stage that carries a 32-ft. diameter revolve. There are eleven rows of seats, on well stepped levels, on the main floor: access is by side gangways. And three balconies, each carrying one row of paired seats, step forward into the auditorium. A fourth balcony carries stage lighting and projection equipment. It is a very attractive scheme that ought to dislodge some of our prejudices about galleries, and I hope some such arrangement will be put in a theatre for actors instead of for tractors.

Which brings us to stage lighting. Nothing that I have said about sightlines and seating for new theatre forms arises from principles in any way new or different from those governing the proscenium theatre. The same applies to stage lighting. No new principles are involved. However, dozens of plans and drawings of theatres with new forms of stage have been shown to me, by experienced architects as well as by students, and nowhere else can such ignorance have been displayed as in the stage lighting arrangements. Even engineers, qualified and experienced in lighting enclosed stages, seem to lose their senses when faced with an open stage. The fault they commonly commit is to place all the stage lighting directly over the acting area. This will illuminate the tops of the actors' heads, sink their eyes in shadow and generally give all but prone figures a ghoulish appearance. What comes over architects when they devise such lighting? I think the answer is that they have never grasped the basic principles of illumination and panic when denied the familiar equipment on bar 1, bar 2, and bar 3 of the enclosed stage. So let us go over the old basic principles and arrive, a bit unexcitingly, at reasonable recommendations.

First of all, stage lighting and sightlines are connected. In a theatre you only see what is lit and you only see it if light coming from it, travelling in straight lines as it does, can reach your eyes uninterrupted by opaque obstacles.

Secondly, stage lighting comes from sources that, in comparison with daylight, are small and restricted, so that a three-dimensional object, such as an actor, lit from a single source or from a single direction, is illuminated on that side but left in shadowy darkness on the other side.

Thirdly, light and shadow are comparative terms and we automatically adjust our eyes to see, at any moment, objects illuminated within a limited range. A dimly lit object may be clearly seen in the dark, but appear to be in shadow if surrounding objects are brightly lit (as anyone working with actors in front of a cyclorama must know).

Normally stage lighting is required to illuminate the actors and scenery while leaving the audience in shadow. For open stages floodlights and compartment battens have too wide an angle of spread and would illuminate stage and auditorium alike. But spotlights can be more precisely directed. On an open stage, then, lighting instruments must be spotlights.

In terms of light alone, the most efficient way of illuminating an object on stage would be to shine a light along the line of sight of the spectator, as though you were to sit in the theatre with a powerful torch. There are several objections to such a procedure. Since there are many people in an audience, fairly widely spread, it would be difficult to find a way of mounting spotlights so that they themselves did not get in the way of sightlines. And either shadows cast by actors would loom large and be a distraction, on, for instance, an end stage, or light would shine across the acting area into the eyes of other members of the audience, inevitably on a centre stage. Finally, illumination along the line of vision tends to make three-dimensional objects look flat and to reduce the perception by the spectator of depth and distance. So mere efficiency is not enough. If we gradually move the light source to increase the angle formed by its light to the object and by the light from the object to the spectator, shadows are introduced. These restore the appearance of solidity and distance; and a complex object such as the human face remains acceptably recognizable until this angle grows beyond about 60°. This angle can be taken as a rough maximum. The shadow effect created by this lighting

angle can be more or less cancelled out by a similar light moved
out to a similar angle but in the opposite direction along the
same plane. With two sources of light we thus have control
over the amount of illumination and the extent of shadow. In
the theatre, the angle of lighting will, because of the lateral
spread of the audience, tend to be critical in the vertical plane,
but there is virtually no limit to the distribution of lighting
positions in the horizontal plan. Thus we can easily move
spotlights in the horizontal plane in order to get efficient
lighting. But movement in the vertical plane is limited, and
because of the difficulty of lighting from a fairly low angle we
sometimes have to light from below eye-level, this being the
purpose of footlights, which used to be more fashionable than
they are today. The main problem with footlights for an open
stage is that they would light up the auditorium, and even a
few spotlights at low level could not overcome the difficulty.

The choice of vertical lighting angles round an open stage is
bound to be restricted. However, fairly satisfactory results can
be obtained by distributing light sources round the object, even
at the same vertical angle. The minimum vertical angle
depends on the disposition of the audience. When spectators
are on the opposite side of the stage from the light source and
fairly close to it, this angle can seldom be less than 30 degrees,
and it is usually more. A raised stage makes for added difficulties, and this is one of the reasons why open stages are not
much raised and centre stages not raised at all. Our choice,
then, lies between 60 degrees and 30 degrees.

For most practical purposes, actors on the open stage should
be illuminated by spotlights distributed round the acting area
to illuminate them at a vertical angle of between 30 degrees and
60 degrees, and both extremes of vertical angle will be used.
For an end stage the lateral spread may be limited if you wish,
though backlighting will be useful. For a centre stage, a
logical lateral distribution of three lights at angles of 120 degrees
can be commended. A thrust stage can be lit by making a
compromise between these two. Obviously a systematic
selection of light sources must be made. And in addition to
lighting the actors it may be necessary, on an end and a thrust
stage, to illuminate the background independently: again, no
new principles are involved.

But even when lighting a cyclorama or skycloth at the back of an end stage, although battens and floodlights are often used, soft-edged, fresnel spotlights will serve better. A cyclorama should not be lit from too close because this causes hot spots near the light source. And I question the sense of lighting a cyclorama from fairly close and from above: this is the common arrangement on small enclosed stages, and the extra brightness it gives to the top of the cyclorama seems to me to be distracting and unhelpful. There is no need, on any stage, to put up with this, unless you really don't care or you are afraid to tackle entrenched ignorance and prejudice (I don't blame you). Instead, I suggest you keep your cyclorama lighting as low as you can manage, and indeed light it from below as well as from above and from the sides if you can.

If you have an architectural background, a problem that is virtually insoluble arises: how do you light actors under balconies, or within inner stages? Some well directed, low-angle spotlights from the auditorium may help, but they may cause trouble in other parts of the acting area whenever their beams are interrupted. A large number of baby spotlights under the front edge of the balcony will be essential. But matching light under balconies with light on the main stage will tax your control operator.

Having decided where to place your spotlights, make sure that you can get at them easily for adjustment and for maintenance purposes. It should be possible for the operator to move a spotlight easily and to see all the various places that it may from time to time have to illuminate. Don't count on getting at spotlights from a ladder: this is a primitive and clumsy technique. In a small theatre most of your spotlights will be in the ceiling, which can be made up of catwalks, or even itself floored over and ranged with lighting traps. Galleries, too, can provide for stage lighting positions. A theatre should never be designed without including accessible positions for spotlights and the designer should check with an expert that the positions are as good as possible.

Consider that a theatre is a building designed to house actors and audience so that the latter can see (and hear) the former. The architect's job is to provide a place for each and the means of seeing (and hearing). In other words, stage lighting is a primary architectural requirement, and to design a theatre means designing the lighting. The common practice of designing a house which is supposed to be a theatre, and subsequently trying to fit in the lighting, usually leads to distressing results even after bitter quarrels between architect and technical consultant.

Perhaps I have been too dogmatic about stage lighting. Let me go back. Stage lighting is absolutely unnecessary, provided performance takes place in the open air, in daylight. It is not essential to light the acting area and leave the audience in the dark. I daresay someone will want a theatre where the audience is as much illuminated as the actors. But it is not likely. I believe that a playhouse requires the conditions we have so far considered, and that an open stage in particular benefits from the help that concentrated light on the acting area gives to focusing the audience's attention on the actors. There is bound to be some spill, but this is no reason to be careless in siting spotlights. Too much spill into the auditorium leads to a restless theatre, where the audience finds difficulty in watching a play. Stage lighting should be a positive aid to actors, not an obstacle to the audience. So if your theatre goes contrary to these precepts, I hope you have good reason.

## DATA

*Section A—Sightlines*

| | |
|---|---|
| Eye-level of seated person | 3 ft 8 in. |
| Top of head | 4 ft |
| Difference | 4 in. |

*Section B—Seating*

| | |
|---|---|
| Optimum distance, back to back | 3 ft |
| Optimum distance, adjacent centres | 1 ft 9 in. |
| Width of gangways | 4 ft 6 in. |

*Section C—Raised Stages*

| | |
|---|---|
| Maximum height | 3 ft 6 in. |

*Section D—Unraised Stage*

| | |
|---|---|
| Raise front row to | 7 in. |
| Each remaining row by increments of | 1 ft 2 in. |
| Thus, second row | 1 ft 9 in. etc. |

*Section E—Number of Rows*
 Maximum number for linear projection     20
 Maximum number for organic projection    10

*Section F—Spotlights*
 Strand pattern 123 can take either 250 or 500 watt lamp, with beam angle adjustable between 15° and 45°
 Strand pattern 223: 750 or 1,000 watt lamp; 15°–55°
 Strand pattern 243: 1,000 or 2,000 watt lamp; 15°–50°

## IX

## SIZE, SCENERY, AND COST

THE decision of size springs from innumerable considerations, some of which we can now examine. How big
should a theatre be? From hints already made, I suggest that
a thrust stage is probably best in a large theatre seating
between 1,000 and 1,500 people, a centre stage in a small
theatre seating between 400 and 1,000, an end stage in one for
100 to 400, and an adaptable theatre is best for 50 to 200. These
are rough figures and may be tossed aside for a particular
design and for the sake of considerations other than theatre
form.

Most people would, I guess, want to build a theatre as big as
possible. We are all impressed by sheer size and it can call up
the kind of amazement appropriate to a theatre. But what are
the limitations to size? Firstly, members of the audience
should be able to see and hear. Forget those Greek theatres:
they were built in the open air which was not then cluttered up
with the noise from the neighbouring metropolis nor of the
aircraft flying to and from it. They used their theatres for a
few days in the year only, when the weather could be relied on
to be fine; and if it wasn't fine, who cared in the midst of a
semi-religious festival? Such conditions do not press on us
nowadays. We roof our theatres over to protect us from the
elements and the man-made din: inside these sheds, acoustics
and sightlines present us with special problems that are
accentuated by bigness. For us, then, there is virtue in a degree
of modesty: stretch your sightlines and test your acoustics to
topmost pitch, and then be sensible and consider building a bit
smaller than that.

The size of a theatre must be regulated, too, by the estimated
size of the potential audience. Begging a host of questions, I
would like to reckon as follows: in any town, suppose that we
intend to run a professional stock company in a playhouse that
puts on a different play each fortnight, presenting it for a
dozen performances, then I hope we could rely on six per cent

of the population to come to each play. So a population of
50,000 would give us an audience of 250 per performance, on
average. Allowing for some performances to be better attended
than others, a capacity of about 300 might be sensibly proposed.
This may be optimistic, but I firmly believe that every town
with a population of 50,000 or more ought to have its own
professional theatre. However, a capacity of only 300 may not
seem to be a viable proposition for a professional company.
Again, I am sanguine, particularly if a non-scenic theatre is
used. Further, I firmly believe that a fully professional company
should be able to prosper under these circumstances without
subsidy; subsidy should be looked on as a helpful extra, not as
a necessity: it means that the size and number of salaries can
be increased or an occasional lavish production be staged or an
extra publicity campaign be launched. Certainly, when public
money must be accounted for and when there is comparatively
little money to give away for the purpose of promoting drama,
the most deserving companies are the small ones, the pioneering
ones and the experimental ones. If a long-established, big
company, in a major city, cannot pay its way, then it probably
does not deserve subsidy, and should be the first candidate for
closure in any rational scheme.

A professional theatre should be designed so that the expenditure of presenting plays can be met by income from ticket
sales. It is not always possible to do this, but the objective is
worth aiming at. I do not want to ride financial hobbyhorses
so hard as to obscure artistic considerations, but I must confess
that I am shocked by the dependence of so many theatres in
England on subsidy. For the most part, subsidy as at present
distributed does not support artistic endeavour so much as
underwrite extravagance, waste and indolence in our theatre:
the vices, one might have thought, of the commercial theatre.
I might even tolerate extravagance if there were any indication
that it has a byproduct of creativity, or waste if it were a
necessary part of originality, or indolence if it were essential to
the dramatic temperament. But no such thing. Our standards
of presentation and performance are too low to give much sign
of having been helped by subsidy. In England so little money
is available for subsidies to the arts that my complaints may be
considered out of place. Perhaps more money is wasted in

Germany: and, if it is, this does not make waste more attractive to me than good entertainment. The money that we have might usefully be spent in helping experimental work, of which there is so little, and research: thus we might bring our theatre more wholeheartedly into the twentieth century, and even improve our knowledge and use of technical and artistic method. As I see it, subsidy is being used to fossilize out-of-date notions of theatre and to ensure that what happens on stage can never be more than a nostalgic, harmless, and indulgent ceremony to attract the middle-class, middle-aged and middle-brow sector of a sleepy society.

In contrast, I hope you are attracted to new theatre forms because you enjoy watching actors who bring their full creative talents to the moment of performance, because you trust that drama can help in the process of enlarging our humanity, and because you want to face today's ideas in art as well as in life, since the one is a reflection of the other. I hope you like the thought of an aggressive theatre, arising from fresh imaginative concepts, and that you are not content with second-hand goods: plays performed by others, performances copied from others, as well as costumes worn by others and scenery used by others. Well, an aggressive theatre is not likely to get subsidy, so plan without it.

By my calculations, Manchester and Liverpool, should have enough theatres to provide about 4,000 seats each night, Leicester, Edinburgh and Leeds 3,000, and Hull 2,000. Each of these cities should have at least three playhouses in addition to an opera house (which would be used for opera, ballet, pantomime and by visiting companies such as the National Theatre and the Royal Shakespeare). The playhouses themselves should be various and top priority ought to go to a thrust stage with an auditorium for a thousand or more, and a centre stage with an auditorium for four or five hundred; throw in another form of theatre for good measure and to make sure standardization does not creep up on us. None of these playhouses should require subsidy, though the building of them might well be paid out of municipal funds.

Smaller towns would have fewer theatres but the principle should be considered that for an audience potential of anything over six hundred it is better to build two playhouses than one.

We should thus expect a greater variety of theatre forms besides a wider selection of plays.

Of course, the wider neighbourhood may swell your potential audience in these days of mobility (so much practised as to be increasingly unpractical), but if you rely on this don't forget the importance of car-parking space. There may come a moment when the car-park question suggests that you give up that splendid site in the centre of town and move into the suburbs or beyond where land is cheaper and you can spread yourself, and not just on car-parks but on backstage space and space for audience amenities as well. The main advantage of the centre site was supposedly that people could see your fascia; but could they? In all that welter of Woolworths, Boots, Marks and Spencers, C. and A., the Odeon, the Gaumont besides the Town Hall, Public Library, Police Station and Market? Few people happen to be passing a theatre at the right moment to say on the spur of the moment: "Let's go inside." The whole business of promoting a theatre, of selling seats, needs, I believe, thorough re-examination but my guess is that a well designed theatre out of town is a better proposition than a cramped one in the centre.

What kind of shows will you present, and what kind of company will play in your theatre? If you are considering one of the new forms of stage, you will cut yourself off from touring companies. Although the National Theatre has played at Chichester and might therefore consider a visit to another thrust stage, it would be unwise to rely on this. A new form of stage should depend on a resident company, be it a professional stock company, an amateur society or a school or college group.

If a resident professional company is expected to play at the theatre it will make full-time use of it, and there is no sense in supposing that occasional visiting companies can be fitted in, nor that the theatre will be available to amateur groups whenever they want it; unless, that is, there is a huge sum of money available to pay the professional company at times when they are not using the theatre. And this sum might be better spent on building a second theatre so that both demands might be satisfied.

In most theatres, administration is a more or less routine office job. It has its oddities, and it may meet the public to sell

tickets in the booking office, or, dressed in dinner-jacket, to
say "Good evening" to the customers. Administration is based
on the assumption that plays are written (mostly bad plays),
actors act, and people come to performances. In a big metropolis, or where a theatre has been established for a long time,
such an assumption may be justified. But your new theatre is
likely to be in another situation: a theatreless town, where,
perhaps, there used to be theatres that have now closed; surely
administration here has a special task? It is to promote the
theatre, to sell tickets, to get the audience in, and to make sure
that money is not spent on stage unless it materializes at the
ticket office. I see little sign, in England, that anyone cares
much about promotion or does anything vigorous to bring the
public into the theatre. Perhaps we are all convinced that
theatre is a privilege for those in-the-know?

There have been a number of educational explorations,
taking actors into schools, telling the young about theatre, even
performing for the young. I don't want to be too scornful of
all this as it may do some good to someone, sometimes. But
drama for the young is a special and limited branch of theatre,
misunderstood by most professional theatre people. School
forays, like taking plays into prisons, may momentarily excite
a captive audience, and I doubt if they do much else: from an
educational point of view drama is probably being misused, and
from a professional point of view watch out that your programme of plays does not deteriorate in order to accommodate
plays that are supposed to be suitable for the young (another
field full of thorny problems).

Many theatres in America, such as the Guthrie Theatre, now
arrange their ticket sales so that by far the largest proportion
of tickets is sold on subscription. Thus the likely income for
the season is known before the productions are mounted. In
any English city, only a few people will have been to the theatre,
know where it is, have any idea what goes on inside. The
dissemination of information is usually left to a few posters,
swamped by the displays of Guinness, Shell, Walls, and
hundreds of other good things to buy; to a local newspaper
critic who must show off his knowledge of dramatic art by
cavilling at your productions, or his lack of knowledge by
praising them inanely (nobody except you reads his column

anyhow); a classified advertisement or two, which probably
never got anyone into the theatre; and some handbills that
have limited distribution and usually do no more than keep
your regular customers informed. Not only are most people
ignorant of your theatre, the few who pretend to know something about it have often managed to seize hold of myth: in
the foyer of any provincial repertory theatre you are likely to
hear, after a performance, someone remark "Not bad, for
amateurs." Someone will ask you what the actors find to
occupy themselves with during the day, while another person
tells you how clever it is to make up all those words every
night. If anyone, who has never been to a theatre before, dares
to try a visit for the first time, the whole enterprise is discour-
aging, from the ritual of getting tickets to the lack of welcome
or guidance anywhere. Theatres have come to assume that
audiences know how to behave, and no thought is given to the
novice. At the Opera House in Manchester there is a sign in
the auditorium announcing "Gentlemen and Buffet," but
initiates know that the buffet has been long closed: only
beginners are fooled and their blushes are a guarantee that they
won't trouble the theatre again. Theatregoing has become too
stupid a ritual to allow of new audiences. But if you contemplate a new form of theatre you may be wise to look for some of
your audience among that 90 per cent of the population which
supposedly doesn't at present go to the theatre, and your
theatre administration should bring as much creative and
original thinking to the job of getting an audience as your
actors do to entertaining it.

Of course your best selling point in the theatre is good acting,
and without this to sell tickets is more or less fraudulent; but
how to get the public in to see for themselves? I suggest, for
instance, that the administrative staff of a theatre might include
half a dozen door-to-door salesmen whose main purpose would
be to tell people that the theatre exists, in such and such a
street, and that the actors' performances give great pleasure.
When interest has been aroused, a trial sample may be appropriate. And it will be important that the tentative spectator,
arriving at the theatre, is looked after and made to feel all the
excitement of the occasion without any sense of being got at
either by cultural evangelists or other chicanery. The salesman

must be a perfect host. In fact, in my own experiments, I have preferred to use the term *theatre hosts*. Our theatre host should visit houses, hotels, offices, factories, schools, colleges, and talk to individuals, the people who would enjoy theatre if they were to come. A number of theatre hosts should divide the town into different sections, and each have his section and get to know its people. They should get to know him, and feel at ease on seeing him in the foyer. But your theatre host should join in the campaign to sell tickets. There is much to commend subscription to a season, which will be attractive to any *aficionado* as well as to the novice.

I think ticket prices should reflect your attitude to the public, not your attitude to the design of the theatre. At least, the design of the theatre should be such that all seats give an equally good opportunity for full enjoyment of the play. Perhaps standing room might be at a reduced price, but I think standing should mainly be available as overflow room for particularly successful shows, so that anyone booking late may still have a chance to see the play even in some possible discomfort. The price of tickets should be reduced for bulk bookings by parties and for students, pensioners and other hard-up people. By all means, at the other extreme, arrange a fashionable day, if possible, by inviting the mayor and a celebrity or two from the world of television, and double the price of tickets. Serve a special dinner after the show, include it in the ticket price suitably adjusted. But make sure that such special occasions do not scare away someone who wants to visit the theatre for the first time. And never charge for programmes.

Use the theatre as much as possible for talks, trade shows, conferences, and concerts. Every person who comes in through the doors should be so pleased with the building that he will want to come again.

Let me stop there. I cannot pretend I know how, starting from nothing, to win an audience into the theatre. It is a subject that fascinates me and I wish I could find a few enthusiasts to discuss it with. But my friends are either successful and complacent, or subsidized and above such concerns. And I don't want to pass on to you theoretical notions without a practical basis in which I have actual experience.

It is sensible to work out your budget on the assumption that your theatre will be occupied to 50 per cent of capacity on average each night, but don't be satisfied until you have passed the 90 per cent mark and have saved enough money to build an additional theatre.

I have assumed that you are running a professional theatre and that you have a stock company and put on plays at regular intervals of two weeks, performing every night (except Sundays) throughout the year. None of these assumptions is basic. A semi-professional theatre, run on the lines of so many community theatres in the United States, might be welcome here in England. You may wish to engage artists especially for each show, though a new form of theatre is likely to benefit from the shared experiences of a team of actors forming a stock company. And you may like to run your plays for a limited season, and in repertoire. It has recently become fashionable for provincial repertory companies to schedule plays in repertoire, keeping several plays in hand instead of presenting each play in succession. Many theatres find that a repertoire presents new problems in the storage of scenery, which may lead to the use of a store away from the theatre with consequent extra labour and transport. The cost is considerable. Not only do these new problems worry the National Theatre and the Royal Shakespeare company in London, but even so new a theatre as the Nottingham Playhouse cannot easily afford its repertoire; and its director, John Neville, has expressed a wish that the theatre held 200 more people to foot the bill. However, the new forms of theatre can readily do without scenery and thus deal satisfactorily with repertoire. Even the architectural background that can be adapted for each production makes sense instead of nonsense out of repertoire. At the end of a season of theatre in the round in Scarborough we had seven plays in repertoire and presented each at successive performances in a single week: a strain on the actors, perhaps, but not on the technical staff (of two people) nor in any way on the budget.

The desire to achieve a homogeneous effect on an audience from the stage leads to preference of a small theatre to a large one. How small? For linear projection, an actor can probably reach across sixty feet without too much distortion at either end of the distance. Organic projection needs closer contact between actors and audience, and thirty feet thins communication about as far as one would tolerate.  If possible, don't stretch either to breaking point.  Note that these distances do not completely control audience capacity;  and while a thousand or more people can be got round a centre stage within thirty feet, only a few hundred could be arranged to face an end stage within the same distance.

Most of us assume that an opera house must be large, seating about 1,200 people, and for a conventional opera house this is probably true.  The size is not really determined by economics, since opera seldom survives without subsidy, but depends on the proportion between stage spectacle and the audience, as well as on the overall volume appropriate to singers and orchestra.  But is it right to assume that opera and ballet cannot develop from their nineteenth-century mould?  In answer one must call to witness such twentieth century operas as *The Turn of the Screw* and *The Medium* where Benjamin Britten and Menotti have begun to explore, once again, chamber opera; and the work of the Western Theatre Ballet or of Merce Cunningham, where modern dance has reneged from the gigantic school of Diaghilev.  The operas and ballets, the singers and dancers are there to assure us that there is something to be said in favour of small theatres even for these branches of dramatic art.  No one would propose sentence of death on the Royal Opera House in Covent Garden, but if you want opera and ballet in your provincial town you may be able to get it without having to build a white elephant.  Your opera and ballet on, say, a centre stage will give you considerable pleasure, and may even earn a reputation that will bring people from all over the world to see them.

The tendency to build a theatre as big as possible needs watching carefully.  In the end, there seem to be many reasons for building a theatre on a smaller scale than might in fact be possible.  Above all, it is better to play to full houses in a small theatre than to empty seats in a large one.  It is better to save your profits and build anew, than to count your losses and close your theatre.

New theatre forms align themselves in various ways in relation to scenery.  At one extreme, an end stage can make as much use of scenery as the enclosed stage.  At this extreme, though, there is not much point in building an open stage at

all since an enclosed stage will certainly be able to handle the
scenery much more efficiently and for no more cost. At the
other extreme, a centre stage need have no scenery whatever
and not even properties, if you insist. But this is probably
taking drama out of the theatre altogether and into someone's
drawing room—or cellar. Most theatres will come between
these extremes. However, a centre stage makes virtually no
demand on scenery, while other open stages may use a permanent architectural background, an architectural background
capable of rearrangement, a cyclorama with projection
and some scenic units, or, finally, more or less conventional
scenery.

Let us look at the question of scenery for the open stage in
more detail. Firstly, whereas the function of an enclosed stage
is precisely to utilize scenery, the open stage implies that the
theatre is ready for performance without scenery. This impli-
cation does not have to be met slavishly, but a well designed
end stage will be immediately usable and the theatre itself will
provide a locale perfectly suitable to any play. There will be
nothing that must be concealed, neither in the way of spaces nor
of machinery. At best, an architectural background may offer
some positive aids that from time immemorial actors have
found useful, such as various entrance ways, levels and traps.

Entrances are important. They should not be doors. An
architectural door is difficult to see through or hear through
and therefore an actor will have difficulty in timing an entrance:
besides he may be carrying properties, wearing a complex
costume, or be required to make his appearance onstage
running. Entrances onto the stage should be open archways,
and they should give on to a passage which provides room for
the actors to wait, out of sight of the audience, for their cues to
go on stage. From the passage there will be doors to the
backstage areas, but these doors should not be seen by the
audience. Entrances on to an end or thrust stage should be
provided at the back of the stage, where there might be three
(at either side and in the centre), and right down stage on
either side, where for the thrust stage they will be vomitory
entrances. For no form of theatre is there any particular virtue
in requiring the actors to make entrances through the audience;
it should be possible for them to do so for a pantomime

production or children's play, but for all normal adult theatre actors' entrances need to be as easy to negotiate as possible without attracting special attention. If an actor wants to attract attention, that is another matter, and he will always be able to do so. Many thrust stages are designed without proper consideration for entrances at the front of the stage, and in use they tend to impose a dullness on the actor's movements or force him to make trick entrances through the audience. Consider the possibility of having a number of alternative entrances that may be convincingly blocked when not required. In this context, don't forget that a trapped floor can provide entrances from below in selected places on the stage.

Instead of an architectural background, the end stage can make good use of a cyclorama. Of course, while the architectural background to be effective must closely define the acting area, the cyclorama will be convincing as a sky background only if removed from the limits of the acting area so that the actors shadows do not fall on it. This gives a clue to the relationship between the walls and ceiling of the theatre and the cyclorama: the theatre should appear to open out into space. In the space between acting area and cyclorama, a ditch should be built so that lighting can come from below. This is most important. A cyclorama should have the most light at its lower reaches, not at the top. But lighting will also come from above. In both cases a reasonable throw is desirable so that the spread of light may be fairly even. Consider painting the cyclorama a medium shade of grey-blue. If it is too light it will tend to be painfully dazzling when lit and to dominate the acting area at all times. If it is too pure a blue, most other colours, whether in light thrown on to it, or in costumes before it, will suffer in comparison. Also consider having a very rough concrete finish rather than the usual smooth plaster. The roughness will return multidirectional light very well, it will provide an unsympathetic surface to hands which otherwise so often leave their mark on what is meant to be the limitless sky, and it may be both more resistant to the inevitable accidental knocks and more easy to patch up afterwards. Note that, all things else being equal, an end stage with a cyclorama will take up more floor space than an end stage with an architectural background.

A plaster wall, specially designed to serve as a screen for projected scenery, has much to recommend it. The device has been thoroughly explored by James Hull Miller, and mention of it has been made on page 83. To be effective, the screen wall must be at the back of a deep acting area, a projector position must be provided in the correct location, stage lighting for the actors must be arranged so that it does not interfere with the projection, and all the audience should be able to see all the screen wall. It is not a cheap alternative to a cyclorama, but it is a very versatile scenic device.

Now for more conventional scenery. Let us start off with a dogmatic statement which we can subsequently chisel away if necessary. Whereas scenery on an enclosed stage makes use of a suspension system to let in units that mask the top of a setting, and side units to mask wing spaces from the audience's view, the open stage makes use of free-standing scenery over which and round which the audience may see as much as is lit for their benefit. The stage setting on an enclosed stage virtually has to fill completely the picture frame, though this does not hold good for the rare stage with a complete quarter-sphere sky dome. Of course, free-standing scenery is common on any stage, but while the masking of backstage spaces of an enclosed stage calls also for a collection of borders, and wings, the open stage does without them. Free-standing scenery needs no suspension lines to support it, and no framework to define its limits, but it stands on its own, surrounded by space.

The implications of this basic fact should be absorbed by your scenic designer, and I doubt if he will find the absence of wings and borders in any way a limitation. I guess, rather, that he will dance for joy. It may be difficult to put a box set designed for an enclosed stage on to an open stage, but it is just as easy to design and make a set for the one as for the other, and the fact that we often see the distressing results of the first method on our open stages should not blind us to the validity of the second.

To eke out one's necessarily limited theatre-going, great pleasure can be got from looking at pictures of stage designs and photographs of settings. Newspapers, magazines, books and the loose collections of friends all add to the fun. I am intrigued by the way artists of the nineteenth century depicted the stage.

They showed not the scenery as they saw it but the impression that the scenery was supposed to give to the audience. You might expect such glossing over the cracks from the designer himself, before translating his intention into flats and ground-rows, but hardly from an artist making an objective account of the actual scene. Cartoons frequently tell the truth about scenery, though, as about so much else. One may conclude that, at least in the nineteenth century, audiences took their scenery very seriously. Sketches and photographs of stage settings always have an advantage over the real thing because they are flat. We see the picture composed as the designer meant it to be seen. This is true only of settings for an enclosed stage, of course, where even the setting contributes to what I have called linear projection. Introduce the idea of organic projection to scenery and a photograph begins to have limitations. You can sense this if you look at the more unorthodox designs of Adolphe Appia, that great artist who believed so passionately in three-dimensional theatre, brought fully to life with the aid of stage lighting. Appia might have had more productions in the theatre if open stages had been available for him. His designs seem frustrated by their two-dimensional reproduction, and, as two-dimensional pictures, are less convincing than designs really intended for two dimensions; hence the neglect into which so much of his work has fallen. A comment on this suggestion can be derived from seeing what happens when your scenic artist, designing for the enclosed stage, is forced to deal with three-dimensional reality, as he is, for example, in most exterior scenes. Designs for these often look convincing enough on a sheet of paper but in execution they too often fail because of the difficulty of making a fair transition between space and the proscenium frame. In realistic scenery the problem is more intense and more complex. In a production of *The Cherry Orchard* or *The Three Sisters* by the Moscow Art Theatre, from Stanislavsky's time to the present day, the interiors are wonderfully credible, but the exteriors are absurd, with their inadequate tree-trunks, the overhead foliage trying to pretend it isn't a border, the dense forestation of the wings, and comic humps trying to disguise the flatness of the floor. It is all so obviously canvas and a bit of chicken-wire, fine for a pantomime, but quite out of key with the interior settings. Of course, the open stage cannot, any more than the enclosed stage, give you realistic exteriors, and it shouldn't try: it can give you open space, for interior and exterior which the actors create in passing—a technique steadfastly relied on by Shakespeare.

In economic terms, scenery is costly, the storage and manipulation of scenery on stage require expensive spaces, and the manufacture and moving of scenery are additional items of expenditure. A non-scenic theatre need not face any of this expenditure in construction nor in running costs. Open stages may all be well used as non-scenic stages. But, if you want a bit of scenery to brighten up your productions you may introduce it on to the open stage, though scarcely on to a centre stage, and more completely on an end stage, and the more you have, the more your costs will mount. Although elevator stages or truck stages could be adapted to turning an open stage into a fully scenic theatre, we have no examples of this; and it seems a contradiction in terms. The best fully scenic theatre seems inevitably to involve an enclosed stage of some kind. Except that, on an open stage, scenery must be free-standing, it is in no important way anything other than more or less conventional scenery.

During the nineteenth century many theatres burned down. Sometimes a theatre fire, even if it did not destroy the building, caused serious loss of life, through panic often enough. Safety regulations have been devised, in the light of actual experience, to prevent loss of life. Scenery has been a notable fire hazard, particularly when stored over the stage, suspended from the grid ready for use. But such scenery must be light-weight and cheap, and it is no use building it of metal or asbestos. Various so-called fire-proofing techniques have been devised for flats, cloths, and draperies. They usually do no more than make the material respond tardily to flame: the scenery burns in the end, but the delay enables the theatre to be cleared before the holocaust, or gives time for firefighters to save the day, particularly if the scenic area can be isolated both so that the fire and smoke shall not be seen by the public and so that draught can be controlled (in fact a lantern window over an enclosed stage ensures that the stage itself will become like a factory furnace!). Fire-prevention officers, who are responsible for passing verdict on the safety of a theatre so that it can get a licence to open, usually have doubts about the use of conventional scenery on an open stage where there can be no safety curtain. They take into consideration the time taken to clear a full house; the number and placing of exits, siting of gangways, and the total number of people allowed in the theatre at one time. But scenery remains a hazard. Two fresh considerations must, however, be taken into account. Firstly, when safety regulations have become so efficient that fires seldom occur, it becomes increasingly difficult to revise regulations pragmatically: it would be silly to relax them and invite disaster, but new precautions can only be tested under laboratory conditions that take time and cost money. Secondly, new materials are in fact being devised. Some of them turn out to be disappointing, but others may in the end prove their worth. If you want to use scenery on an open stage you may find restrictions placed on the overall design of your theatre, on the amount of scenery you are allowed to use, on how you mount scenery, how you build it and the materials you build it of. There are no set rules. You and your chief fire officer must come to your own conclusions. And you may get useful information on recent research into new materials from the A.B.T.T.

Scenery handled on the stage floor needs extra wing space adjacent to the stage. It may be simply struck from the stage, flat by flat, and stacked against a wall or in racks nearby, or whole sets can be shifted on trucks or on a revolving stage. Consideration must be given to shifting scenery during a play, and from play to play, and the theatre should be designed so that all shifting can be carried out at a single level. Workshop, paintshop, stores, and wing spaces should all be at stage level. If scenery is made outside the theatre, loading level should be at truck height as well as at stage level. All doors, too, must be tall enough to allow the tallest piece of scenery normally used to pass through with room to spare, and wide enough to pass the biggest of units likely to be used on stage.

A scenic theatre needs storage space. Workshop, paintshop, and store should each be allocated an area of about three times the actual acting area. In addition, wing space (the storage space immediately adjacent to the stage) should have an area equal to or more than the acting area: the wing spaces and acting area together form the stage of a proscenium theatre.

Even if you decide to build a non-scenic stage, provision must be made for costumes and properties. The policy of the theatre may be to hire costumes, thus reducing the need of storage space. But even hired costumes need care and maintenance and a wardrobe room remains essential. Besides, nearly every theatre acquires at least a few special costumes of its own and these will require storage space. If the theatre is to make its own costumes, in addition to considerable storage space and a good wardrobe room, a laundry room should also be planned, with extra facilities for dyeing and drying lengths of material. Properties, too, eat up space; a workshop and storage should be allowed for. Most theatres want to store some furniture. A centre stage makes extra demands on costumes, properties, furniture and other three-dimensional units, and therefore needs more workshop and storage spaces than you might expect.

Back to considerations of safety. Workshops and stores should be separated from stage and auditorium so that fire hazards are not shared. This may mean extra thickness to walls, double doors of special quality, or it may mean independent and adjacent buildings.

Dressing rooms for the open stage need be no different from those for the enclosed stage, and information about their requirements can easily be obtained. But I want to put forward an unusual suggestion, though it applies only to small theatres. Whereas most people take it for granted that it is better to have many dressing rooms than few, and that small rooms to take one or two actors are better than large ones (a preference based on the accepted notions of star dressing room and of chorus room), I consider that there is much to be said in favour of a single dressing room for the whole company. The room should be divided by a low partition so that men and women can have the essential privacy expected by both sexes. The advantages of the single room include the sharing of conversation and information; if a company of actors is to appear on stage, working together as a team, they will be helped by tuning up, as it were, together in the dressing room: actors must be sensitive to each others' capacities and moods, and, rather than push them on stage where they must create their characters without awareness of the persons beneath, they should share the process of going from actor to character; making allowances, perhaps, for a partner who is unusually ebullient tonight, or tired and depressed. The two parts of the dressing room should open on to a common area, serving as a green room. Conditions of this kind were forced on the company in Scarborough's Library Theatre, and, I believe, did much to make the standards of performance higher than one might expect from a young company, overworked, under-paid, and, many of them, inexperienced. I would hesitate to put forward the idea to a thoroughly experienced company, but I have a suspicion that it might still be valid: most actors would at first be very angry at finding a single dressing room in a new theatre, but they might come to recognize its advantages.

An important factor in pricing a building will always be the overall floor area. In a theatre the area required by auditor-ium, facilities for actors, audience and administration remains constant for any given audience capacity no matter what form of theatre; the variables are the stage itself, scenic spaces and accommodation for technicians, and these vary with the form of theatre. In general open stages make more modest demands on these variables than enclosed stages, and this is why they are less expensive to build. In particular, the less use made of scenery the less space occupied by stage, scenic spaces, and technicians. Hence, theatre in the round can be taken as the least expensive of all theatre forms.

Of course, the demands of scenery affect not only capital out-lay in building a theatre but also production and maintenance costs, as well as the salary bill. A non-scenic theatre is also economical to run.

In conclusion, though, I hope no one ever builds a theatre in the round only because it is cheap. The attractions of each form of open stage are positive, and affect not only money matters but the whole business of acting and of enjoying a performance; it is the latter that will, of course, govern our choice.

# BOOK LIST

THERE have been few books to cover the ground of new theatre forms, but a good deal of useful information can be easily got from the following:

BOYLE, WALDEN P., *Central and Flexible Staging* (University of California Press, 1956). This is a well-illustrated book, dealing with simple problems in simple terms.

JOSEPH, STEPHEN, *The Story of the Playhouse in England* (Barrie and Rockliff, 1963). Although covering familiar ground, the book does attempt to give unusual forms of staging proper historical prominence.

JOSEPH, STEPHEN, *Theatre in the Round* (Barrie and Rockliff, 1967). The subject is the central stage, and mainly in England, but it deals with many questions of acting and production that arise in all forms of open stage.

MILLER, JAMES HULL, *The Open Stage* (Hub Electric Company, 1965). This booklet has been published by an American firm to advertise lighting control equipment, but it contains useful plans and drawings of theaters and some excellent articles on lighting and scenery.

SOUTHERN, RICHARD, *The Open Stage* (Faber and Faber, Theatre Arts Books, 1953). An attempt to state the claims of what here we have called the thrust stage.

SOUTHERN, RICHARD, *The Medieval Theatre in the Round* (Faber and Faber, Theatre Arts Books, 1957). The book deals only with the central and peripheral staging of the middle ages, and primarily with a single play: *The Castle of Perseverance.* But it is a fascinating study.

SOUTHERN, RICHARD, *The Seven Ages of Theatre* (Faber and Faber, Hill and Wang, 1962). A wide-ranging historical account of different theatre forms.

ABTT, *Theatre Planning* (Association of British Theatre Technicians, 1964). A technical guide for theatre architects, containing some useful articles about different forms of theatre.

# INDEX

The theatres listed in the following index are those chiefly dealt with in the book. Where possible each theatre has been entered under the name of its town or city, except in the case of London theatres, which are entered by name.